A Heral

Martin Dudley was born in Birmingham and educated at King Edward's School. He studied theology at King's College, London, and has a doctorate in theology. Ordained in Wales, he has been a parish priest for twenty years and is now Rector of St Bartholomew the Great, Smithfield, in the City of London. A Fellow of the Society of Antiquaries and of the Royal Historical Society, he has edited and contributed to a number of books on theology, history and liturgy including, most recently, *Humanity and Healing* (DLT) and *Ashes to Glory* (SPCK).

A Herald Voice

The Word of God in
Advent and Christmas

Martin Dudley

Published in Great Britain in 2000 by
Society for Promoting Christian Knowledge
Holy Trinity Church
Marylebone Road
London NW1 4DU

British Library Cataloguing-in-Publication Data

A catalogue record for this book is available from the British Library

ISBN 0-281-05280-8

Typeset by David Gregson Associates
Printed in Great Britain by
Omnia Books, Glasgow

Contents

For Michael

Preface

Many voices call to us in the Advent and Christmas liturgies. Some cry out from the depths of our humanity, expressing our sense of being oppressed, weak, and limited. Others call from somewhere beyond, summoning us to the horizon, affirming our worth and significance. Between them, between the sense of being limited and ineffectual and the glimpse of unimaginable glory, comes the process by which God chose to dwell with humankind. In this process God remains God, the sovereign Lord, the last and incomprehensible mystery, and we, hearing the word of God, knowing ourselves as those who are addressed, find a new God-given dignity and strength. As we hear the word of God we know at last who and what we are.

My own experience is that we can also forget who we are. I find that I have become the person who attends to the children's needs, who pays bills and tries to keep track of money, who goes to work and achieves a fraction of what I set out to do. I become someone who isn't there but is always coming from somewhere or going to somewhere else, or who lives partially in the other worlds created by the electronic media or by the book. Standing among my books I sometimes pick up a volume that has been untouched for some time, often one of the books that I read when I was a student. Alongside theology and some philosophy, especially Plato, I read a large number of books by French writers (in translation), wrestling with Jean-Paul Sartre and Albert Camus but really feeling most comfortable with André Malraux, the writer who became General de Gaulle's Minister of Culture. He was a fascinating figure, an adventurer, an intellectual, a poet and novelist, a leader of the French Resistance, a practical politician, and a man with a great vision of how modern media made the world's art available to everyone. The photograph, he thought, made it possible to have an art gallery in every home. He would have loved the CD-ROM and the worldwide web. 'In front of Malraux,' said André Gide, 'one doesn't feel very intelligent.' But Malraux was not a remote figure. He was passionate about living and he realized that any lasting achievement requires time for its development, and that the imponderable factors – the accidental, the absurd, the quixotic – are the fabric of life. What he had to say significantly shaped my own approach to living.

At the time when I read these books, twenty-five years ago, I was passionately concerned with the nature of human existence. As time went by I experienced it more and reflected on it less and found myself drawn increasingly into planning, fund-raising and administration. Still I was involved in crucial moments of people's lives, and none more important than conception, birth, the achievement of adulthood, marriage, sickness and death. Giving up reflecting upon what these mean is partly the result of intellectual laziness but partly a version of that defensive mechanism, foreshortening of vision, that H. E. Bates describes bomber pilots using in *Fair Stood the Wind for France*. I stood, I suppose, once too often in a wind-swept churchyard gazing into a deep hole and saying 'earth to earth, ashes to ashes, dust to dust'.

When I read certain passages in the Bible or find that, in writing a sermon, I must clarify the meaning of some words or follow through the development of some doctrine, I castigate myself for this idleness. I hear Wisdom crying aloud in the street, raising her voice in the market, calling from the city wall, 'How long, O simple ones, will you love being simple? How long will scoffers delight in their scoffing and fools hate knowledge?' (Proverbs

1.22) and I begin again to write in a sort of philosophical notebook and ponder the nature of human existence. But as Jesus ben Sirach says, 'The wisdom of the scribe depends on the opportunity of leisure; and he who has little business may become wise' (Sirach 38.24). The necessities of work and family life limit the possibilities for reflection. We are fortunate as Christians within the liturgical tradition that the liturgy itself affords us moments of insight and the possibility of recalling who we are and how we are addressed, of 'having in remembrance' the mystery of salvation.

As Advent begins it sounds an alarm clock, calling us to wake from sleep and to attend to things eternal without neglecting that which is passing away. It culminates in the joy of the Nativity even as it looks beyond the Nativity to Christ's return in glory. Its traditional themes are death, judgement, hell and heaven, and we must at least glance at them as we rush towards our own Christmas celebrations and be ready to hear the voices that not only challenge our approach to living but offer us a better way. Advent is a time to reflect, not penitentially, as in Lent, but with hearts full of hope and longing.

This little book may repay some of the debt I feel towards the seasons that have long stirred me and filled me with delight. At the same time I would like to use it to acknowledge with deep gratitude and affection the constant support and encouragement that I have received in over twenty years of friendship from Father Michael Thompson, now Rector of St Mary and St Martin, Stamford, in Lincolnshire.

Martin Dudley

St Bartholomew the Great, Smithfield

Acknowledgements

Except for those otherwise noted, biblical quotations are taken from the Revised Standard Version of the Bible, Old Testament © 1952, New Testament Second Edition © 1971, Division of Christian Education of the National Council of the Churches of Christ in the United States of America.

Rights in Britain and the Commonwealth to material from The Book of Common Prayer, 1662, are vested in the Crown. It is reproduced by permission of the Crown's patentee, Cambridge University Press.

T. S. Eliot, *East Coker*, and 'Journey of the Magi' from *Collected Poems 1909–1962* © 1963, T. S. Eliot with permission from Faber & Faber Ltd.

Hymns are reproduced from *Hymns Ancient and Modern Revised* (1950) by permission of the publishers.

The English text of the Great 'O-antiphons' is taken from *The Roman Breviary – An Approved English Translation* © Benziger Brothers, New York.

Wedding prayers are from *Documents of the Marriage Liturgy* © 1992 The Liturgical Press, Collegeville, MN, with permission.

Quotations from the Fathers, except where otherwise referenced, are from Henry Ashworth Henry, OSB (ed.), *A Word in Season* © 1973 Talbot Press, Dublin.

Elizabeth Poston's translation of Angelus ad virginem in *The Penguin Book of Carols*, is reproduced by permission of Campion Press.

1

The Many Voices of the Liturgy

As a young child I always delighted in the sort of learning games in which you had to play a role. It began with what was called music and movement. In a draughty school hall the teacher would ask us all to be trees swaying in the breeze or else we might have to be soldiers marching along or lumberjacks felling a tree. And later we learned to use our voices and to understand that we could convey meaning by the quality as well as by the loudness of what we said. Such school activities were marked by creativity. Oddly, perhaps, that approach did not extend to reading Scripture in the Baptist Church where I grew in Christian faith. Clarity was all important and it was somehow presumptuous to employ the methods of the theatre or the poetry reading. The Bible was its own best interpreter. I was to learn that this was not a view everyone shared. At sixteen or seventeen, I was asked to read a lesson – Isaiah 40.1–11 – at a school carol service. Our Chief Master, an Anglican cleric and distinguished English scholar, did not approve of the way I read. 'You have an ecclesiastical monotone,' he said, and set about teaching me to read in such a way that my voice conveyed the sense and meaning of this wonderful passage. He taught me to be – for that moment at least – a herald voice, to be the one who cried out in the wilderness. It was a revelation to me for it alerted me not only to the different voices that the reader might employ for different passages but also to the different voices that were already calling from Scripture and, as I was to discover when I moved from the Baptist Church to the Church of England, within the liturgy.

The Book of Common Prayer was also something new to me. I encountered it first at Evensong in Christ Church, Oxford, when I was seventeen. Baptists were then used to having a hymn book and a Bible and nothing else. I found this little book confusing and fascinating and like choirboys of old I ended up reading the Table of Kindred and Affinity and various other curious lists and tables when I should have been concentrating on the service. The rubrics – the instructions to the minister and people that used to be printed in red – are always interesting. Almost the first such instruction in the Book of Common Prayer, in the Order for Morning Prayer, is for the minister to read some sentences of Scripture 'with a loud voice'. My first vicar took this absolutely literally and boomed them out. A little further on the minister is instructed to 'say the Lord's Prayer with an audible voice'. It was a major concern of the Reformers that the words, rendered from Latin into English, should be heard – that the minister should be heard by the people and that the minister, clerks, and people should all be heard by God (for they are all to say the Lord's Prayer 'with a loud voice'). The loud and audible voice is contrasted with the mutterings and mumblings of the unreformed Roman Mass and its secret prayers. When you look carefully through the Prayer Book you find a stream of instructions to priests and ministers to say this thing or to speak to these persons in this way. We also find godparents bringing children for baptism and those to be confirmed or married being charged to answer audibly so that all may hear the promises made.

Use of the voice was not only a matter of concern to the Reformers. One of the little books that guided hundreds of Roman Catholic seminarians as they prepared to say Mass for the first time was *The Sacred Ceremonies of Low Mass*, by Felix Zualdi and rendered into English by one James Murphy (in its last pre-Vatican II edition of 1961). It had a chapter concerned with different tones of voice. There were, it explained, two means of speaking: secretly and aloud. For the portions of the Mass said secretly the priest was to 'pronounce the words so that he can hear himself', but not be heard by others, even those around the altar. The other parts, those said aloud, were to be said in a 'clear and intelligible, but moderate and grave, voice, such as will excite devotion'. The priest was also warned against undue haste, excessive slowness ('which would weary those present'), too loud a tone and too low a tone. I am reminded of an instruction in a thirteenth-century text from the house of Augustinian Canons at Barnwell, near Cambridge. It required the precentor, who was responsible for all that was sung in the Mass and Offices, to start the antiphons and intone the psalms and said that 'whatever he begins he ought to pronounce deliberately, with softness and sweetness of voice' (*cum suavitate et dulcedine vocis*). That such concern is taken over the voice to be used in worship shows just how important it is. It can be a means of proclamation or a means of concealment, depending on whether the speaker declares words loudly or whispers them. It can set the whole tone of the liturgy, guaranteeing its joyful or penitential nature.

DEFINING THE VOICE

What exactly do we mean then by 'voice'? Though we know what we mean if we say 'I heard a voice' or 'I have lost my voice' or something similar, it is very difficult to define the word. Any dictionary definition begins with sounds or a whole sequence of sounds produced by the vocal organs and swiftly moves to vocal sound as the vehicle of human utterance or expression. Our voice expresses what we are, but we can put on a false voice, disguising the way we sound. The voice that is heard is not necessarily the authentic voice. It is not surprising then that, when instructing monks on the behaviour appropriate to the presence of God and his angels, St Benedict says that the mind must be in harmony with the voice.

The voice, and not just the words it utters, has an affect on those who hear it. We swiftly pick up on the way in which something is said, hearing in the voice itself excitement, joy, panic, love, or warning. Voice is closely related to language and even when we learn another language we may not easily grasp what different ways speaking imply. The voice can seduce us into accepting what would otherwise be unacceptable. One astute commentator on the phenomenon of Adolf Hitler noted that his voice – unmistakably Austrian in origin – was enigmatic to German audiences; its manner of speech strangely vertiginous and synthetic. His speeches were rhetorically weak and devoid of intellectual content but he had an amazing capacity to convey feeling. As J. P. Stern remarks in *Hitler: The Führer and the People*: 'The Greeks are known to have valued euphony above all else in speech, which they thought of as "beautiful song". The Italians and French have a similar attitude; their great orators are singers. The German is won over by feeling ... he looks for a man of faith, of character.'

THE WORDS OF THE LITURGY

Liturgy has used set texts for more than 1500 years and those texts made abundant use of the forms of speech already familiar from the public and private reading of Scripture. The officiant does not normally write the liturgy and ministers have rarely, until today, needed to provide their own suitable words. Extempore prayer is alien to the liturgical tradition. The words of the liturgy are shaped by use. Like rough-hewn stone beneath the mason's chisel, they have been rounded by constant praying, by repetition, by being taken to the heart. Liturgical change is, in consequence, difficult, for it almost always involves change in language, in the words of the liturgy and the way in which they are spoken.

The liturgical voice takes many forms and has many tones. For the medieval liturgy, celebrated with the full participation of ministers and people, the voice was always one that sang or chanted. Liturgy involves dialogue. This is obvious at the simplest level when texts involve dialogue between minister and people using versicles and responses. This is most clear when a single voice or the choir, the schola, enunciates the word and the assembly replies. It is less clear in antiphonal singing, when the verses are sung alternately across the choir. The hymn, sung by the whole assembly, does not have the character of dialogue at all. In addition to the human voices a greater dialogue takes place between the heavenly and the earthly, the divine and the human. The human voice, praising God and making intercession, is replying to the divine voice. The divine word is addressed to humankind. Hearing involves more than just recognizing the spoken words, for as Jesus reminds us in the parable of the Sower the word of God is like a seed. It is scattered over a wide area but it must take root if it is to bear fruit. So the word can be heard by many, perhaps by all, but true hearing involves the word being implanted within the person.

For utterance to make sense, sound must be punctuated. The punctuation is provided by silence. The word must issue into silence if there is not to be an incomprehensible babbling. Silence is followed by speech; speech by silence; and in dialogue, discourse and conversation, silence is followed by further response. This pattern exists in the divine discourse more perfectly than in human discourse. It also provides a fundamental structure for the liturgy. This is a deep underlying structure essential to liturgical performance.

But there is more to voice than volume and silence. The voice, singing or speaking, can convey a sense of joy or sorrow, it can acclaim and implore, declare and demand, teach and console. Liturgy is a performed text. Sacred space, an assembly and its ministers, ornaments and vestments, together with gestures, tones of voice, and styles of music belong to the essential nature of liturgy. The text is performed within a specific environment, most often called chapel, church, sanctuary or worship space. It interacts with the environment that is specifically intended for its performance. It involves a repertory of symbols. These include the shape, structure and decoration of the liturgical space, the movement, posture and gestures of the assembly and its ministers, and the specific symbolic actions involved in washing, anointing, absolving, blessing, breaking bread and sharing the cup. The ritual of the liturgy delivers up its secrets only when celebrated in community. Sung or spoken, the text that is performed on a given day, at a given time, and in a particular celebration, takes its place in a context defined by its position within a cycle of liturgical celebrations, by the type of literary genre employed, and by its relation to other texts and the mode of their performance. We see this most clearly as the days of Holy Week unfold and we sing joyfully in procession, fill with sorrow as we listen to the Passion read or sung, hear the 'Ubi caritas' as feet are washed, behold the wood of the cross, and sing afresh the Paschal Alleluia.

When I say that liturgy is performance, I do not mean something extroverted and self-conscious. The liturgy can be interpreted using the same methods that are applied to secular dramatic productions but it is not a performance in the way that plays are. They primarily operate horizontally, using dramatic methods to communicate with and to involve and engage an audience. The liturgy operates both horizontally and vertically, addressing both the human assembly and the divine presence. It also mediates the divine presence, so that the vertical axis runs in both directions.

THE DIVINE VOICE

The voice that enunciates the divine word addressed to humankind is as varied as any used in human utterance. The voice of the

Lord – *qol Yahweh, φωνη κυριου, vox Domini* – is powerful, full of splendour, shakes the wilderness and resounds over the waters. It crushes the cedar trees, makes the oak trees writhe and splits the flame of fire. But the Lord may also eschew the wind and the earthquake and the fire and be found instead in a still small voice, a faint murmuring sound, in a sound of sheer silence that caused the prophet to wrap his face in his mantle (1 Kings 19.11–13a).

The progression of languages has tended to refine the distinction we make between word, voice, discourse and sound. The Hebrew *dabar* means a spoken utterance of any kind, but it also means a matter, event, act and thing. There is, in consequence, little clear differentiation between word and event, and the word brings the event into being though it is not separate from it. When God creates, he speaks. 'And God said' repeats Genesis over and over again and with each saying there is created light and dark, waters and firmament, earth and seas, plants and trees, sun, moon, stars, seasons, creatures and last of all humankind. All words have special power in the Old Testament world, particularly curses and blessings, but the divine word is of a different order, having a power appropriate to their particular character and an effect appropriate to their particular purpose. A good example of this is found in Isaiah 55 in a text used in the American Book of Common Prayer 1979 as a canticle at morning prayer:

> *For as the rain and snow fall from the heavens*
> *and return not again, but water the earth,*
> *Bringing forth life and giving growth,*
> *seed for sowing and bread for eating,*
> *So is my word that goes forth from my mouth;*
> *it will not return empty;*
> *But it will accomplish that which I have purposed,*
> *and prosper in that for which I sent it.*

The Greek *phone* means a sound, a cry, a voice, as well as speech, discourse, and language. We find it in words like 'telephone' (sound over long distance), 'megaphone' (literally a big sound) and 'microphone' (a little sound). It also provides us with the word *phonetics*. The Latin *vox* means not only the voice but also authority and even vote. We find it in 'vocal', of course. Though the *vox Dei* is the voice of God, *vox sola* is the mere word and *vocalis* means nominal or so-called. The English *voice* has a similar range of meaning but there is a clear movement from the performative nature of the Hebrew word. The English word achieves nothing just by being spoken. Voice is sound but the sound is that of opinion, a report, a statement, and no longer that which brings into being, that which creates. This devaluation has even been carried into the liturgy with the universal acclamation of Bible readings as 'the word of the Lord'. Not every reading gives full expression to the divine word and this uncritical and ill-conceived announcement fails to distinguish the levels at which the word operates and the diversity of texts employed. We can, however, truly say that the word of God is heard in the liturgy.

ADVENT AND CHRISTMAS

I am still excited by the words and tune of the first hymn we sing in Advent at St Bartholomew the Great – 'Hark! a thrilling voice is sounding'. This voice tells us that Christ is nigh and as our days shorten and the night comes sooner every day we are reminded that we are children of the day and must cast away the dreams of darkness. That hymn, a translation of a medieval Office hymn, already indicates the voices to be heard in the liturgy of Advent, and calls us to hear them all. The medieval liturgy was rich seasonal texts contained in antiphons, versicles, responsories, graduals, sequences, tracts, alleluias and tropes (see the appendix for these and other terms). It was capable of expressing many voices in one service and several in the daily round. Today most of us go to just one service a Sunday and miss the resonances created between hymns, psalms and readings at Eucharist, Mattins and Evensong. We may supplement our single attendance in this season by attending a service of Advent music, a Christmas carol service, a Nativity play, and perhaps a performance of Handel's *Messiah*, and so we may, thankfully, be exposed to more of the voices. I began by identifying and naming nine of them emerging from two strands – one concerned with Christ's first coming and the other with his coming again in glory.

The first is a voice that carries a double message of judgement and of hope. It is that of Isaiah, the Advent prophet, promising the chosen people a definitive judgement and a cause for joy. The second is closely related to it. It is that of John the Baptist. Again it carries two messages, that of the good news of the coming of Christ and with it the call to repent. I have called this the penitential voice for we not only hear John's call to repentance but we respond to it and our own voices declare our sorrow for our sins. Isaiah and John both declare their faith in what is to come and the liturgy gives voice to this sense of expectation based on scriptural promises in a series of Magnificat antiphons which, from 16 or 17 December, depending on the number used, greet the coming Messiah in a series of acclamations beginning with 'O Sapientia' – 'O Wisdom that proceeds from the mouth of the Most High'. These are known, from the opening word of each of them, as the Great O-antiphons, and they find a summary form in the hymn 'O come, O come, Emmanuel' and I have called them the expectant voice. To these three may be added the imploring voice that calls 'Come, Lord, do not delay' and looks for the consummation of all things. These four voices, picking up the original meaning of Advent, are directed to the coming of Christ in glory to judge both the quick and the dead.

The other voices are concerned with the incarnation and take us from Advent into Christmas and on, beyond Epiphany, to Candlemas. First there is the announcing voice, that of the Archangel Gabriel addressed to the Virgin Mary, and we hear as well her response to the announcement. Then we come to the silent night and to the utterance in time of the timeless Word of God. This is the voice more powerful than any other voice, the incarnating voice. It is swiftly followed by angelic voices making the Christmas proclamation to the shepherds and offering glory to God in the highest as well as peace to men on earth. Then we hear a voice that cries in pain; this is the cry of the innocents that is so often drowned by our Christmas festivities. It follows the coming of the Magi and Herod's interest in their mission and leads to the death of the children and the flight of the Holy Family into Egypt. The last of the Christmas voices involves a return to the word of prophecy as Simeon and Anna greet the child presented in the Temple and Candlemas brings an end to Christmas. But these categories are not exhaustive and as I wrote I found that I not only heard the voices that I had identified in unexpected ways but also found other voices. There was a constantly questioning voice that reappeared at different stages. There was also a voice that was neither Jewish nor Christian but which incessantly called for attention. It was that of the Christianized pagan or semi-pagan rites that mark winter in the northern hemisphere and that makes itself known in Yule.

DEEP MIDWINTER

The voice of the semi-pagan festivities associated with Advent, Christmas and Epiphany needs to be heard because we cannot just consider the liturgy in isolation. It would be like studying late-twentieth-century Christmas on the basis of Nine Lessons and Carols from King's College, Cambridge, and the publications of the Church of England Liturgical Commission without considering the Trafalgar Square Christmas tree, the Queen's broadcast, and the Morecambe and Wise Christmas special. We can, however, give little space to them and none at all to Christmas trees and cards and the trappings of the Victorian celebration, much as I love them. If we do attend to these non- or pre-Christian voices – and they are heard at some unlikely moments in liturgy and devotion – we must also hear the preachers who condemned them. San Bernardino of Siena, for example, early in the fifteenth century, deprecated the pagan element in primitive popular customs which had gradually become incorporated in some of the feasts of the Church. 'The very feast-days', he said, 'on which our spirit should turn to God are obscured by pagan ceremonies.' Two or three of them from across Europe deserve to be noticed.

One of the most popular practices in Tuscany was the ceremony of the Yuletide log or *ceppo*, which was placed on the hearth on Christmas Eve by the head of the family and decorated with gifts and coins. He called out: 'Give it to drink! Give it to eat!' The *ceppo* was then anointed with oil and blessed, and sometimes other smaller logs, representing the children of the family, were placed beside it in the fire. Sparks were drawn by striking the log with a flint or other metal and omens were drawn from them, while the number of sparks that had been drawn were supposed to show the number of years that the head of the household would still remain alive. All this was probably a survival of fire-worship at the winter solstice, when the fire's aid was called upon, on the shortest day of the year, to promote the growth of the new sun. To this day, writes Iris Origo in her description of the world in which San Bernardino lived, in remote country places, people believe that the *ceppo* blazes 'to give light to *Gesù Bambino*'. In some places strict rules applied to the log: it had to be received as a gift, or else to be from a tree on one's own property, or it could have been found but it could not be bought. When it was kindled, last year's log had to be used and it was never permitted to go out by itself but was always to be extinguished.

A number of Advent practices are related to the deepening of winter and to the placing at one time of New Year on Christmas Day. It was believed in England that during the whole of Advent fairies, witches, goblins, and malevolent spirits possessed their most formidable powers of annoying good Christians until they were quelled by the 'hallowed and gracious time' of Christmas Eve. Many Advent and Christmas practices are intended to defend people against these malign forces. The Christmas customs of the Anglo-Saxons almost certainly included the yule-log, mumming, the hunting of small animals and birds, the wassailing of fruit trees by pouring ale on them while incantations were sung and the use of evergreens as decorations intended to protect from evil spirits.

Another tradition relates to the Thursdays in Advent. Some old writers mention a custom of boys and girls going about in crowds on the Thursday three weeks before Christmas, crying 'Advent! Advent!' and wishing their neighbours a happy New Year. They were given money and fruit. In Upper and Lower Bavaria and rural parts of South Germany the three Thursdays are called 'Knocking Nights' (*Klopfelnächte*). The children go out dressed in masks and recite rhymes beginning with 'Knock ...' (*Klopf an*), and they use various methods to make as much noise as possible. It was thought that the noise – made with cracking whips and ringing cowbells – frightened away the evil spirits, and the children were rewarded by being given sweets, fruits, nuts or money. Although Christmas is not, as many say it is, primarily for children, children have always found a way of profiting from it!

There were also the voices of the Advent and Christmas saints, not only Stephen and John and the Holy Innocents, but also Nicolas, Barbara and Lucy, the martyred Thomas Becket and Pope Sylvester, whose day falls on New Year's Eve. We cannot give the same attention to every voice and some will remain unheard, but what is important is to know that there are many voices to be heard and each Advent and Christmas to listen intently for those not yet heard.

Part 1

Advent

2

The Questioning Voice

Through the Advent and Christmas liturgy we hear many questions being asked. God asks Adam 'Where are you?' Mary asks 'How shall this be?' John asks, through his disciples 'Are you the one who is to come or are we to wait for another?' The Magi ask 'Where is the child who has been born king of the Jews?' But the first question that concerns me is one put to Jesus by Pontius Pilate the Governor in St John's account of the trial, passion and death of the Lord. This may seem a strange place to begin, but there is not a distinct ending and a distinct beginning in the liturgy. We have rather a series of cycles and as we think about them we may recall T. S. Eliot's words in *East Coker*, the second of the *Four Quartets*, 'In my beginning is my end'. As the liturgy comes to its conclusion, so it starts us off again, and as it begins it already has the end in sight. As we begin Lent, we know that Jesus' death will lead to his resurrection. As we begin Advent, we know it leads to the celebration of Christ's birth even as it looks beyond it to his coming again in glory.

One of these liturgical cycles that is most familiar to us is that of the seemingly endless Sundays after Trinity or after Pentecost. The number of Sundays was and is variable and in the old system readings left over from after the Epiphany might be used to fill up any vacancies. The post-Trinity period always ended, however, with the same set of Sunday propers. In the Roman and Anglican traditions this 'Sunday next before Advent' had an eschatological flavour. That is to say, it looked to what in Greek was called the *eschatos*, the end of all things. And it used a well-known collect, 'Stir up, we beseech thee, O Lord, the wills of thy faithful people'. It was often known as 'Stir up Sunday' and became associated with the making of Christmas puddings!

Today the Sunday at the end of November before Advent begins is often celebrated as the Feast of Christ the King. The feast was instituted by Pope Pius XI, on the last Sunday of October, in his encyclical letter *Quas primas* of 11 December 1925. By creating this new feast the Pope wanted to make a solemn proclamation of the social dominion of Christ over the world and to show that organizing social life as if God did not exist leads to denial of religious belief and to the ruin of society. The introit of the Mass – *Dignus est Agnus* (Worthy is the Lamb) – begins with the Lamb upon the throne, and the whole Mass shows Christ's kingship to be both of this world and of the world to come. The collect speaks of all the nations of the world, torn apart by the wound of sin, being made subject to Christ's gentle rule. Unfortunately, some modern versions of the feast make Christ the 'King of hearts' rather than the king of our world, of nations, structures, and institutions as well as individuals.

Jesus was called 'king' on a number of occasions but there is one particular point that enables us to understand what this might mean. It is the question put to Jesus by Pilate. You may, as I said, think this a strange place to start in a book about Advent and Christmas, but let me explain why it is important. When the new altarpiece in the Lady Chapel at St Bartholomew the Great was first unveiled someone looking at the lovely, bright infant Jesus enthroned on his blessed mother's lap commented that the altar cross cast a shadow across it. He suggested that I remove it. He had not realized that the cross does cast a shadow across the life of Jesus from Bethlehem onwards and that it cannot be removed, figuratively or really. The child Jesus is enthroned on his mother's lap. One day he will reign from the tree of Calvary.

My friend, the poet and writer Virginia Rounding, expressed this wonderfully in a set of new verses that she wrote for Bishop Reginald Heber's hymn 'Virgin-born, we bow before thee':

Blessed she who, in a manger,
Kept thee warm and free from danger,
And watched while kings and shepherds came
To gaze in awe and praise thy name.
Blessed was the breast that fed thee;
Blessed was the hand that led thee;
Blessed she who, in her arms,
Protected thee from all alarms.

Blessed she who, in thy growing,
Watched with joy and sorrow, knowing
Her Child was God the Father's Son,
Who prayed each day: Thy will be done.
Virgin-born, we bow before thee:
Blessed was the womb that bore thee;
Mary, Mother meek and mild,
Blessed was she in her Child.

Blessed she who heard thy teaching
And believed in thee, beseeching
The wedding guests to do thy will
And of new wine to drink their fill.
Blessed she who, fears defying,
Stood beside thee in thy dying,
And with the women waiting there
Bore thy last hours in silent prayer.

Virgin-born, we bow before thee:
Blessed was the womb that bore thee;
Mary, Mother meek and mild,
Blessed was she in her Child.
Blessed she who, in her weeping,

Held thee lifeless as though sleeping;
Blessed she who cradled thee
In death, as in thine infancy.

ARE YOU THE KING OF THE JEWS?

Over the head of Jesus on the cross was a superscription. All the
Gospel writers agree about what it said. John alone tells us that it
was written in three languages – in Hebrew, Greek and Latin. On
most paintings of the crucifixion there are just four letters: INRI –
meaning *Iesus Nazarenus Rex Iudaeorum* – Jesus of Nazareth, the
King of the Jews. The latter part of chapter 18 of the Gospel
according to St John and the first 22 verses of chapter 19 are
concerned with the idea of Jesus as a king. Pilate, unversed in the
religious peculiarities of the first-century Jews, can grasp the idea
that Jesus might be a rebel, opposed to Roman rule and laying
claim to kingship. This is a sufficient reason for him to be
executed. And he stays with this idea no matter what the Jews say,
because it justifies his action. He wavers for a moment when the
Jews speak of Jesus as the son of God but in the end he settles for
executing a failed usurper. Pilate did not understand or perhaps
did not want to understand his conversation with Jesus. Jesus did
not deny that he was a king or that the idea of kingship expressed
some part of what he was but at that same time he made it clear
that his kingship was not of this world.

In Greek, Pilate asks whether Jesus is *ho basileus ton Ioudaion.*
Basileus is the Greek word for king, for one having regnal power.
It passes over into Latin – where king is *rex* – in the word *basilica*
which was initially the place where authority was exercised by a
magistrate and subsequently became the title applied to church
buildings modelled on Roman basilicas. The underlying reference
to regnal power was not lost and the apse of a basilica was
decorated with a great mosaic of Christ the King. In the same way

that we can see the cross as both the cross of glory and the cross of sacrifice, so we need to hold together two images of Christ as King. The one shows Christ in majesty, wearing the robes that would have adorned the Roman and Byzantine Emperors, with a crown upon his head, seated on a throne, set against the gold background of eternal glory. The other has Christ in the purple robe of kingship wearing a crown of thorns, mocked by the soldiers; Christ hanging upon the tree, the superscription above his head. The Church knows that it cannot hold to one, either one, without the other.

Jesus preached the coming of the Kingdom of God from the very moment he began is ministry. He did not attach his teaching to any of the prevailing hopes. He did not say that the Romans would be ejected from Israel and a new theocracy established. He did not entirely express his idea of the Kingdom in terms of eschatology, of the end of all things and the coming of a new heaven and a new earth. He spoke of it openly but he spoke in parables. Over and over he says 'The Kingdom of heaven is like this: there was once a king . . .' and so he provides his hearers with powerful images. One thing is entirely clear, that the promise of the coming of the Kingdom is related to the deepest human hopes and aspirations and that the key words are peace, justice, freedom and the fulness of life. We must constantly recall Jesus' answer to Pilate, 'My kingship is not of this world', and reject any authoritarian concept of rule, any idea of kingship that suppresses or contradicts human freedom. It is the constant temptation of religion to impose its principles on others. We have seen that in much of Christian history and we see it as well in conservative Judaism and in fundamentalist Islam. Israel discovered that having a king was not all it seemed to be. The Romans associated the very word 'king' with tyranny and there was never a king in or of Rome after Tarquin the Proud.

Jesus has told us that the greatest amongst us must be the servant of all and that makes it the more extraordinary that we constantly disregard what he says and separate power from service. Accepting divine rule involves concrete acceptance of this principle and the most concrete step is the recognition that it is in God that we live and move and have our being. It is, I find, almost a cliché in my preaching and writing, for I find I have to say it over and over again. We do not live because of our own power. We do not sustain ourselves in existence. We are dependent on and grounded upon God. And God, the ground of our being, is revealed in Jesus as the living God of love and we exist and are sustained because of that love. Jesus makes kingship a service undertaken in love and that becomes the distinctive feature of the Kingdom.

What does this mean for us, in practice, as those who affirm the kingship of Christ? Can we do more than reduce it to a set of pious words about love, peace and justice? I believe we can. We can do it by acting in faith and in deliberate opposition to egotism, self-seeking, self-will, self-advantage and self-importance. If it is these things that shape our lives then we are denying the kingship of Christ. What we have to do, by faith and by God's grace, is to act out of love, for Christ's victory means that, contrary to all appearances, it is that which is done in the world out of love that endures. The kingship of Christ opens up as a reality for us an alternative to transforming the world by violence or escaping the world by pacifism or non-involvement. Transformation and humanization are affected by what I can only call, borrowing others' words, the violence of love, a love that knows no constraints and refuses to be intimidated.

The service that Christ's kingship demands is not easy. He doesn't call us at this point to abandon all and follow him into the wilderness. He calls us to express love's transforming power in our daily living. This is much harder than abandoning the world. We are to stay with it and yet not ultimately to be of it, knowing that we belong to the kingship that is not of this world. We live with the tension between the enthroned Lord and the crucified Lord. We live on the boundary of this world and the world to come. We are to live as strangers, pilgrims, aliens, building up treasure in heaven not treasure on earth and at the same time be truly and really present where we are and, being there, be agents of Christ's love. No one said it would be easy, but Christ teaches us and shows us that it is possible.

COME TO THE MARRIAGE FEAST

In one of the parables in which he speaks of the nature of the Kingdom, recorded in Matthew 22, Jesus tells of a king who gave a wedding banquet for his son. One needs to be careful when dealing with monarchs. *Debrett's Etiquette and Modern Manners* is a book that stands on my reference shelf along with dictionaries, a thesaurus, various Oxford companions and a dictionary of quotations. I rarely refer to it but I happened to a few years ago when I decided to brush up on royal etiquette in preparation for a visit by the Queen to St Bartholomew the Great. I find that with reference books I soon drift off the subject I first thought of and move on to others, more obscure, more interesting, and so I discovered how to reply to an invitation from the Queen or Queen Mother. It is a royal command and should be answered as such. You respond by writing that you 'have the honour to obey Her Majesty's command' and if you should find it necessary to decline then, says Debrett, the reason must be given and it should be a substantial one!

The king in Jesus' parable issued a summons to those on the list of the invited, but they did not treat it as a command, quite the opposite – they simply would not come. Kings are used to obedience and so the king thinks perhaps that there has been a misunderstanding and so sends a further invitation telling them that everything is ready for the marriage feast and they are to come. At this point the parable leaves behind any semblance of reality. Why should they kill the king's servants just because he brings an invitation? How can a wedding feast still be ready after the king has massed his troops, destroyed the murderers, and burned their city? And why is a man who comes to the feast bound hand and foot and thrown into outer darkness? How do we explain these odd details?

The feast is an image of the end, the culmination of history, that has been prepared by God. The marriage feast points us in particular to the Son of God as the bridegroom in the Revelation to John, and the parable looks back on the sweep of the history of salvation from the sending of the prophets to the final judgement.

God has prepared, says Isaiah, a rich feast, a feast of vintage wines and of elaborate dishes, and the invitation, the divine and royal summons, has been ignored. The servants who carried the invitation – the prophets, John the Baptist, Jesus himself, and, in due course, the apostles – are ignored by some and abused by others. Jesus specifically charges the religious leaders with the murder of the prophets and the spilling of innocent blood, and warns of the consequences of rejection and abuse. Sodom and Gomorrah, he predicts, will be better off in the day of judgement than those who reject the teaching of his disciples. The violent attack on the city, though a stock motif of Old Testament vengeance stories, must have had a special meaning to the readers of Matthew after the sack of Jerusalem by the Romans in AD 70.

This destruction is not the end. The original guest list is abandoned and anyone and everyone may now come in, both the good and the bad. Again we have an image of future and final judgement. Jesus' own small band of disciples included a betrayer. The Church casts its net far and wide and it must, like the world, be composed of a mix of evil and good. The last judgement is the final separation and this is what happens when the king comes to inspect his guests. This ejection of a man for failing to wear a festal garment may seem unfair, but his silence is here an admission of guilt. A garment is, in this parable, an allegorical representation of our spiritual and moral worthiness, as with the fine linen that is the deeds of the saints in Revelation. The individual is at all times to be ready, wearing the right garment, expecting to be called at any time, for this element of surprise, of the unexpected coming of judgement, runs right through the Gospels. This parable is, therefore, an allegory and is intended to show us that the royal command may come at any time, that we should be ready for it, and that when it comes we should reply, without feigned courtesy and politeness, that we have the honour to obey the command of the divine majesty and are ready, eager and willing to share the feast of rich food. Hence the Advent cry 'Sleepers, awake' and the most crucial question of all 'Friend, how did you come here?'

THE LAST GREAT DAY

The first seasonal words of any Advent liturgy said or sung in the pre-conciliar Roman Church were those of the first antiphon at first Vespers of the first Sunday of Advent (on Saturday evening). They were drawn from the prophet Joel (3.18): 'On that day the mountains shall drop down sweetness, and the hills shall flow with milk and honey, alleluia.' The day to which it refers is the eschatological day, the last great day, the day on which the Lord will come. It could just as easily have been a verse from Isaiah, the Advent prophet *par excellence*, who spoke constantly of the coming day and of the coming Messiah. The day had three main features: it was the day of judgement, the day of plenty, and the day of fulfilment. Fear has tended to dominate thoughts of Christ's coming and to displace the other two aspects. It was not by chance that the Anglican divine and spiritual writer Austin Farrer began his book on the Church's year, *Said or Sung*, with his own rendering of *the* hymn of judgement, *Dies irae, dies illa*.

Dies irae, dies illa is a hymn or sequence that used always to be sung at the Mass for the dead. It perhaps derives from a Benedictine rhymed prayer of the late twelfth century which depicts a soul awaiting judgement. The thirteenth century was tightly focused on the theme of judgement and a Franciscan, perhaps Thomas of Celano, one of the first biographers of St Francis, added a new urgency to it. The Latin is terse and vibrant and the many English translations fall to catch the feel of it. Something of its terrifying nature can be caught by listening to Verdi's Requiem or, more powerful still, to the *Grande Messe des Morts* of Hector Berlioz. The *Dies irae* is no longer obligatory in the liturgy but many who read it or hear it read find that it expresses many of their own fears and hopes about death and judgement. Here is one English version:

> *Day of wrath and doom impending,*
> *David's word with Sibyl's blending!*
> *Heaven and earth in ashes ending*
>
> *O what fear man's bosom rendeth,*
> *When from Heaven the Judge descendeth,*
> *On whose sentence all dependeth!*
>
> *Wondrous sound the trumpet flingeth,*
> *Through earth's sepulchres it ringeth,*
> *All before the throne it bringeth.*
>
> *Death is struck, and nature quaking,*
> *All creation is awaking,*
> *To its Judge an answer making.*
>
> *Lo! the book exactly worded,*
> *Wherein all hath been recorded;*
> *Thence shall judgement be awarded.*
>
> *When the Judge his seat attaineth,*
> *And each hidden deed arraigneth,*
> *Nothing unavenged remaineth.*

Faint and weary thou hast sought me,
On the Cross of suffering bought me;
Shall such grace be vainly brought me?

Righteous Judge! for sin's pollution
Grant thy gift of absolution,
Ere that day of retribution

Guilty, now I pour my moaning,
All my shame with anguish owning;
Spare, O God, thy suppliant groaning!

Through the sinful woman shriven,
Through the dying thief forgiven,
Thou to me a hope hast given.

Worthless are my prayers and sighing,
Yet, good Lord, in grace complying,
Rescue me from night undying.

With thy sheep a place provide me,
From the goats afar divide me,
To thy right hand do thou guide me.

What shall I, frail man, be pleading?
Who for me be interceding,
When the just are mercy needing?

King of majesty tremendous,
Who dost free salvation send us,
Fount of pity, then befriend us!

Think, kind Jesus! — my salvation
Caused thy wondrous incarnation;
Leave me not to reprobation.

When the wicked are confounded,

Doomed to shame and woe unbounded,
Call me, with thy Saints surrounded.

Low I kneel, with heart's submission;
See, like ashes my contrition!
Help me in my last condition!

Ah! that day of tears and mourning!
From the dust of earth returning
Man for judgement must prepare him;
Spare, O God, in mercy spare him.

This hymn represents two aspects of the theme of judgement: fear and hope. It may be that fear predominates and that we need to give more attention to hope. A little less fearful is the view expressed in the venerable hymn *Conditor alme siderum* which appears in the Advent Office in the ninth century. It holds together the hope of salvation, the expectation of judgement and the need for protection here and now:

O thou whose coming is with dread
To judge and doom the quick and dead,
Preserve us while we dwell below,
From every insult of the foe.

The idea of fulfilment in Advent is strong and must not be ignored. It runs as a theme through the season maintaining an older idea that the fulfilment of God's promises should, above all, bring us joy. The questioning voice, echoing through Scripture, asks a greater diversity of questions as humankind strives to plumb the depths of both divinity and humanity. The Sundays before the beginning of Advent ask if Christ is a King and, if so, what sort of King he will be when we stand before him. The voices of Advent seek to answer these questions, but the answer is rather unexpected.

3

Waking from Sleep

Adventus Domini, the coming of the Lord, from the Latin, *adventi*, coming, though *adventura*, the Italian *aventura*, means a knightly adventure, such as we find recounted in medieval song and story. The *adventura* can also be *mercator*, the merchant, and in particular the merchant adventurer. *Adventure* has a sense of challenge and excitement, and within it *venture* points to the possibility of risk. Advent is full of risk – risk for Mary, the unmarried mother, possibly outcast because seemingly unchaste; risk for John the Baptizer, who trusted the divine promises and accepted death as the consequence of what he ventured. And is there risk for us? If we invest cautiously, our investment will be safe but the rewards may be slight. If we are more adventurous, if we take a risk, then we may lose capital as well as income. So as Advent begins we may ask what the cost would be if – which is impossible – the promises of God were to fail. No life everlasting, of course, but what is the cost now? A few wasted hours spent in church, but what else? What is there in our life that we would have done or not done or pursued or avoided if Christ had not died and heaven were not promised us? What have we ventured in this life, what have we risked on the basis of God's promises? Advent is a time to consider this.

One evening in mid-Advent a year or two ago I walked from St Bartholomew the Great to my home in the Barbican. The streets, bar and restaurants of Smithfield were full of revellers and party-goers. The sense of excitement among some and of anxiety among others was growing. Cards were arriving, post-office queues were lengthy, last posting days were near, and schools were bringing their celebrations to climax and conclusion. I had just come from the celebration of a liturgy marked by a sense of time-lessness, by the lack of urgency which is a sign of our communion with heaven. As others rushed headlong to the feast, the liturgy was slowly rehearsing the promises of God as set down by the prophet Isaiah, urging us to be patient, and exploring the question of whether Jesus was the one expected and foretold by John or not.

Returning to my study I looked up, in my *Medieval Latin Wordbook* the Latin root verb *excito*, meaning to rouse, to stir up, to awaken. It provides the first word of a number of collects and other liturgical texts that begin *Excita, Domine*. There I also found *horologium excitatorium*, a medieval alarm-clock! I used the link between 'stir up' and the alarm-clock for my sermon the next Sunday morning, the morning my verger overslept and thought the sermon was a deliberate reproach!

The collects urge God to action, stirring him to come in sovereign strength and save his people. But we also are to hear the sound of the Advent alarm-clock and be stirred to greater devotion, to a greater sense of expectation, a greater readiness for the coming of God. The Advent hope in the broader sense of looking for Christ's coming again in glory is not unlike the movement through Advent to Christmas. It involves a delicate balance between excitement and over-excitement. It requires active preparation without premature celebration. It requires patience and the waiting marked by readiness rather than by idleness. The holding in tension of excitement about the promises of God and the recognition that their fulfilment may be some time off – though we do not know when the Lord will come – leaves us in the space between promise and fulfilment, the *mean time*. And our task and challenge is to live in the mean time as those who are destined for the *end time*.

This is not an arid area of theological reflection; it is one of vital significance. It poses vexing questions about the purpose of life – not any life, not life in general, but 'my life'. If the guiding principle of life is the accumulation of wealth, then whatever is perceived as distracting from it must be abandoned. If the guiding principle is service of others, then purely selfish aims and intentions must be deliberately set aside. If we define ourselves as creatures made in the image of the Creator, intended for the worship of God and the eternal enjoyment of the divine presence, passing now through a temporary sojourn on earth, then we will be inclined to order our lives one way. If we consider that human life is the accidental consequence of cosmic interaction and evolution and ends in death, then we will order it in another way. For most of us there are sets and subsets of aims and objectives. Our self-definition as 'Christian' shapes many of these categories and governs, or at least restrains, our intentions and actions in a number of areas, but as we are concerned with food, warmth, shelter, the raising of children, job satisfaction, cultural development, and day-by-day performance of necessary tasks, that Christian self-identity may serve as a foundation, an ideal, and little more, and that may be enough for the mean time.

The *horologium excitatorium* of Advent is intended to wake in us a greater awareness of the divine presence, a greater knowledge of the divine power. It is characteristic of divine forbearance that the alarm call might be drowned out by the sounds of revelry, as a baby in a manger and a criminal on a cross might be ignored. God offers us purpose, hope, and life. In doing so he does not force himself upon us, but invites us to seek him while he wills to be found, to call upon him when he draws near, and in so doing, forsaking evil ways, to be renewed, restored and refreshed, to be given new life in Christ. He does not say that 'religion' and 'piety' are the fullness of living and that we must give up all we enjoy, but he reminds us that separation from the source of life brings death – spiritual, emotional, intellectual and physical death – and he longs for us to call upon his power which provides what is needed to live now, in the mean time, as those intended for and expecting what is to come.

So two themes run in parallel through the historic liturgy of the season of Advent. We may refer to them as a morning theme and evening theme because, in the liturgy celebrated here by the Western Church since the early Middle Ages and in England for just over four hundred years, that is where you would have found them. The Offices of the morning declared appropriately enough that it was time to rise from sleep, that night was past, that God was stirring and the long-awaited day was coming. Let the heavens drop down dew from above, declared the Advent responsory, that the earth might be opened and bud forth a Saviour. The evening gave that expectation a more concrete form. 'Fear not, Mary,' says the Magnificat antiphon, 'Fear not, for thou hast found grace with the Lord: behold, thou shalt conceive and bear a son.'

There is a tendency today to stress only the second theme and even then to mix it up with the secular and material observances of Christmas and with the frankly heathen practices that have become associated with it. Christmas always risks becoming a winter festival rather than a Christian celebration. Even when it is profoundly Christian there is a risk of it being too small, focused entirely on the crib and unaware of the cosmic significance of the coming of Christ. The first theme – Isaiah's theme – maintains and sets forth this important dimension.

O THAT THOU WOULDST REND THE HEAVENS AND COME DOWN

The picture painted by the prophet Isaiah is that of a people whose rejection of God has become habitual and unthinking, a people that has forgotten God. The prophet is addressing the sort of religious complacency that may well be familiar to us. Here is a people who turned from God because of the divine anger directed against them. If God does not like what we do, they said, then we will ignore God. We are in the wrong but we will put God in the wrong. It is our fault, but we will punish him. Such rejection leads to diminishment. Separation from the source of life brings death, but what we see here is loss of vitality, a fading, a loss of rootedness, a loss of reality. The children of Israel are become like the shadowy figures of Sheol, the Old Testament abode of the dead.

The prophet has a solution, however, and it is a truly drastic solution. He longs for God to come again with power, as in the days of old. He longs for the heavens to be torn open and for the mountains to quake at the presence of the Lord. He wants the adversaries of God to know him and to tremble. And so he reminds God of how he acted in the past and challenges him to do so again. A challenge of this sort seems to involve some presumption on the part of the prophet. In some of the tales of King Arthur and the brotherhood of the Round Table, we read of a knight with unknown blazon delivering a challenge, reminding the King and his company of former exploits, and mocking them if they do not respond to his invitation to adventure and to combat. It was, in a way, a ritual performance. There is something of that too in the words of Isaiah. He takes a double approach: he reminds God of previous manifestations of his power and presents the present situation as one that requires similar intervention, asking whether the Lord will keep silent forever.

Such an approach to God can seem like insolence. How dare the creature address the Creator in this way? By what right does the mortal challenge the immortal? By contrast with these words of Isaiah Christian prayer sounds profoundly deferential. It does not blame God; it does not reproach God; it does not say 'how long will you treat us like this?' Yet such blame and reproach is to be found in the traditions of the Old Testament and prophetic voices have not been afraid to rail against God.

God replies to the prophet's challenge. He declares that he has never been absent, has never disregarded the plight of this people. 'I was ready to be sought by those who did not ask for me,' says the Lord, 'I was ready to be found by those who did not seek me. I said "Here am I, here am I," to a nation that did not call on my name' (Isaiah 65.1). The prophet has reproached God but now God reproaches his people for they have forsaken him, forgotten his holy mountain, 'set a table for Fortune' and filled 'cups of mixed wine for Destiny'. That is to say, the chosen people have deliberately forgotten that they are chosen, but haunted by a residual memory have put their faith in Fortune and Destiny rather than in God. And the Advent promise here repeated is that God will not keep silent but will repay, that he will come in judgement and that after judgement comes that new thing that God will perform, a deed of such power that the former things shall not be remembered.

THE TWO COMINGS

Isaiah is clear that we must not sleep for that promised moment is coming, the moment that never has been before and never will be again, the moment when the Lord wills to be found, the moment when he draws near. The Bible tells us of the comings of Christ, of his birth in Bethlehem and of his return in glory, but between those two greater comings there are lesser and more personal events. There are those moments when Christ comes to us in the sure and certain pledges of his love – the sacraments. There are the times in which he comes through his Spirit to dwell with us, and there are those moments of infinite worth when we suddenly and unexpectedly find ourselves attuned, attentive, aware of him and of his love, when he draws near and we know him in a special way. Isaiah reminds us in his prophetic call to Israel of the need to be ready, to strain like the watchman and to see the Lord as he comes, with eyes aided by faith. There are no easily read signs of his coming. It is, by its very nature, unexpected – the coming of a thief in the night.

If Isaiah calls us from slumber, from inaffentiveness, from being submerged in worlds of our own making, Jesus himself warns us of the danger of false prophets. The transition from one millennium to another has been a particularly good time to look out for them. The end of the first millennium was marked by prophecies of doom and redemption. We may not readily understand the apocalyptic statements of earlier generations but we are quite good at producing our own. Whatever the reality, the millennium bug was another version of that, threatening our technological civilization with barely defined dangers and creating a fear which was all the greater for being so ill defined. And so we may say is the fear of paedophilia and child-abuse. Like the anxiety about witches in previous ages, the fear may be much greater than the reality. These and other fears arise and people abandon rationality and flee to what seems clear and secure. Jesus warns us that such responses could lead us astray. Salvation belongs to Christ alone and he assures us that when he comes we will know it. There will be no doubt about it. While there is doubt and fear Christ has not come.

Each Advent reminds us that the purposes of God are still being worked out and that we are part of them, continue his redeeming work, making his love evident in the world, working with the knowledge that, whatever now seems to be the case, it is service undertaken in love that will endure. The Advent voice calls us from our slumbers not to a fearful judgement but to new life and new hope in Jesus Christ. It sets before us the cosmic expectation of a new heaven and a new earth, a new creative outpouring of God's grace and love. It always recalls the concrete expression of that love in Mary's willing obedience and co-operation and the birth in time of the timeless Son of God. We can and should look forward to Christmas with joy. We should also look beyond Christmas to the total fulfilment of the purposes of God in Christ.

REDEEMING THE CREATION

'And the Lord God planted a garden in Eden.' This was how God ordered the natural world that he had made, by planting a garden full of trees pleasant to the sight and good for food. It must have been a garden of great beauty, of wonderful tranquillity, for God himself walked there in the cool of the day. And out of Eden flowed the river that watered the garden and dividing into four it became the Pishon, the Gihon, the Tigris, and the Euphrates. The history of salvation – recounted in Scripture in myth, parable, story and metaphor – is not merely a story about human beings. It is the story of the whole creation, of all living beings, human and animal, but also of the world of trees and plants, and of seas and rivers, plains and valleys, fountains and waterfalls, wilderness and desert. When Adam and Eve were driven out of Eden they found that the very ground itself was cursed because of their sin. The trees give way to thorns and thistles, the ordered beauty of the garden becomes the field, and humankind is destined to return to the dust of the earth.

There are no lyrical descriptions of the natural world in Scripture, no poetic evocation of its beauty. It forms the background to human activity and it is that activity which is highly prized. Cultivation of the land, development, skill in husbandry and agriculture, in building and in decoration is contrasted with the natural world, the unchanged and undeveloped, the desert and the wilderness. The world of human beings is characterized by the city and urban culture, with Jerusalem, the city of Sion, as its zenith, and it is contrasted with the wilderness as the wild place, the place of temptation, the place of danger. That John the Baptist was in the wilderness from his childhood to the beginning of his ministry is an indication of his strength. When Christ – even Christ – ventured into the wilderness, to fast and to pray, he found the Tempter there, the father of lies.

The prophet Isaiah indicates that the wilderness will be caught up in God's salvation, that the dry land will be glad, and the desert rejoice and blossom, blooming abundantly. In other words, that which is the very opposite of the garden, the negation of the garden, shall become as a garden. The abundance of water, so marked in Eden, will become a feature of the wilderness. And this will not happen in any gradual way but quite suddenly – the waters shall break forth in the wilderness.

This same imagery has been applied to the soul, to the spiritual dimension of our humanity. We are told by the great spiritual writers that the soul must be cultivated. If it is left alone it becomes overgrown, with the wrong sort of growth, or else it becomes a wasteland, a desert. The great souls speak of aridity in prayer and of the need for divine watering if prayer is to be fruitful. This is, I think, a helpful image. The soul is something like a garden. It needs weeding, through examination of conscience and through penance; it needs to be planted with the virtues as the vices are weeded out; it needs to be fed with the word of God and with the sacraments. This can all sound a little trite, too fussy for the modern, too tied up with old patterns of devotion and of spiritual direction. It is not a language that comes easily to me, especially as a non-gardener, but I think it is right both to stress the value of spiritual order against disorder and to point us inwards to that which needs our care and which is nourished by prayer and meditation. What we mustn't do is think of our souls or the process of salvation in terms of rows of allotments growing prize vegetables, or neat suburban gardens with herbaceous borders. Isaiah is much more dramatic than that and the saving act of God, the ushering in of the Kingdom, has a degree of suddenness and power that is almost violent; so much so that the fearful need to be told 'Be strong, fear not!'

WACHET AUF

Philip Nicolai (1556–1608) was a Lutheran pastor whose parish was hit by plague between July 1597 and January 1598. His flock was decimated, with 300 dying in July, and 170 in a single week of August. Altogether 1300 died. Nicolai's parsonage overlooked the churchyard and there were 30 interments a day. Every household was in mourning and Nicolai's thoughts turned to death, to God in heaven, and to the eternal fatherland. In the preface to his allegorical reflections on the second coming he wrote:

> *There seemed to me nothing more sweet, delightful, and agreeable than the contemplation of the noble, sublime doctrine of Eternal Life obtained through the blood of Christ. This I allowed to dwell in my heart day and night, and searched the Scriptures as to what they revealed on this matter, read also the sweet treatise of the ancient doctor Saint Augustine [The City of God] ... Then day by day I wrote out my meditations, found myself, thank God! wonderfully well comforted in heart, joyful in spirit, and truly content.*

Out of the meditations came the hymn *Wachet auf* which mingles Isaiah's call to wakefulness with Jesus' parables of the bridegroom. It combines the suddenness of the coming of the Kingdom not with fear, as we saw in the *Dies irae* and medieval Office hymns but with the joy that belongs to those who are ready to receive the bridegroom. The text begins with the familiar German words which may derive from the Wächter-Lieder that were popular in Germany in the Middle Ages, having been introduced by Wolfram von Eschenbach:

> *Wachet auf! ruft aus die Stimme*
> *Der Wächter sehr hurch auf der Zinne.*

Bach set the text as Cantata no. 140 for the Twenty-seventh
Sunday after Trinity and Frances Cox translated it as the hymn
'Sleepers, wake!' with the tune by Nicolai:

> *Sleepers, wake! the watch-cry pealeth,*
> *While slumber deep each eyelid sealeth:*
> *Awake, Jerusalem, awake!*
> *Midnight's solemn hour is tolling,*
> *And seraph-notes are onward rolling;*
> *They call on us our part to take.*
> *Come forth, ye virgins wise:*
> *The Bridegroom comes, arise!*
> *Alleluia!*
> *Each lamp be bright*
> *With ready light*
> *To grace the marriage feast tonight.*
>
> *Zion hears the voice that singeth,*
> *With sudden joy her glad heart springeth,*
> *At once she wakes, she stands arrayed:*
> *Her Light is come, her Star ascending,*
> *Lo, girt with truth, with mercy blending,*
> *Her Bridegroom there, so long delayed*
> *All hail! God's glorious Son,*
> *All hail! our joy and crown,*
> *Alleluia!*
> *The joyful call*
> *We answer all,*
> *And follow to the bridal hall.*
>
> *Praise to him who goes before us!*
> *Let men and angels sing in chorus,*
> *Let harp and cymbal add their sound.*
> *Twelve the gates, a pearl each portal –*
> *We haste to join the choir immortal*

Within the Holy City's bound.
Ear ne'er heard aught like this,
Nor heart conceived such bliss.
Alleluia!
We raise the song,
We swell the throng,
To praise thee ages all along.

(*AMR*, 55)

4

The Voice in the Wilderness

> *On Jordan's bank the Baptist's cry*
> *Announces that the Lord is nigh;*
> *Awake and hearken, for he brings*
> *Glad tidings of the King of Kings.*

(*AMR*, 50)

It is well known that St Mark's Gospel contains no account of the conception or birth of Jesus. The very first line tells you what the whole book is about. It was the first verse of the Greek New Testament I was able to read when, in 1974, I began to study it in the original language. 'The beginning of the good news of Jesus Christ.' 'Good news' in Greek is the *evangel*, from which we get 'evangelist', 'evangelism' and even 'evangelical' but which otherwise comes into English as 'gospel', from the Old English *godspel* – good news, good tidings.

Once Mark has declared his intention, he turns at once to the prophets. He actually says he is quoting Isaiah but he is really quoting one line of Malachi (3.1) and another from Isaiah (40.3). The Evangelist is perhaps quoting from memory or else, because this happens elsewhere, Christians early gathered extracts from the prophets that concerned Christ. Mark's quotation concerns John the Baptizer as the messenger going ahead of Christ, the voice crying in the wilderness, the one who prepares the way of the Lord. And not only does John link us to Isaiah and to Malachi, but also to Elijah, for he looks just like him. He is clothed as a prophet, in camel's hair, with a leather girdle, and lives on locusts and wild honey.

Mark does not tell us what it was that John cried out. Matthew says that he preached saying, 'Repent for the kingdom of heaven is at hand (3.2)'. If that was so, then Jesus begins his ministry in exactly the same way saying 'The time is fulfilled, and the kingdom of God is at hand; repent and believe in the gospel (Mark 1.15)'. If the first Advent voice urged us to wake from sleep, to be alert and to keep awake, the second urges repentance upon us that we might be ready to receive the one who is to come.

John always points past himself to the one who comes after. This is not the good news of John but the good news of Jesus Christ. John looks and sounds like an Old Testament prophet. His is the last voice to tell of what is coming, for in his own day God breaks in upon the world. Jesus said of him that he was a prophet and more than a prophet (Luke 7.26). The Venerable Bede wrote a hymn that begins 'The great forerunner of the morn' to be sung during the Office on St John Baptist's Day, 24 June. It was translated from the Latin by John Mason Neale and, though perhaps little sung today, it appears in a number of hymn books. The fourth stanza draws on the Gospels and summarizes the Church's regard for John:

> *Of woman-born shall never be*
> *A greater prophet than was he,*
> *Whose mighty deeds exalt his fame*
> *To greater than a prophet's name.*

(AMR, 553)

John is not merely pointing to another prophet when he speaks of the one who is coming, and he deliberately sets out the difference between them. The coming one is more powerful and of such a dignity that he, John, is not even worthy to untie his sandals. John baptizes with water but the coming one will baptize with the Holy Spirit of God.

Other Gospel writers will have more to say about John. Luke paints us a vivid picture of the way in which John dealt firmly but sympathetically with those who came to him genuinely wanting to repent but uncertain how their lives might be reformed and renewed. Among these were the tax gatherers and the soldiers. John was less sympathetic to the crowds who came out to see what was new down by the Jordan. He rebuked them with vigour, calling them a brood of vipers and charging them to bring forth fruits worthy of repentance.

The Prayer Book collect for St John Baptist's Day offers a summary of John's role in the plan of salvation and applies his teaching and the example of his ministry to Church and to Christians:

> *Almighty God, by whose providence thy servant John Baptist was wonderfully born, and sent to prepare the way of thy Son our Saviour, by preaching of repentance: Make us so to follow his doctrine and holy life, that we may truly repent according to his preaching, and after his example constantly speak the truth, boldly rebuke vice, and patiently suffer for the truth's sake; through Jesus Christ our Lord.*

John shows us that there is a price to pay in proclaiming good news to the world. For the good news to be received and to bear fruit, the way must be prepared, and preparation begins with repentance. And when we have ourselves repented, when we have applied our best efforts, aided by God's grace, to root out the vices within and without, and to plant the virtues, then we have to turn from ourselves to others. We cannot in faithfulness to Scripture remain silent when the truth is perverted and denied. And we are warned that we may have to suffer, and do so patiently, for the sake of the truth.

John's voice does not sound like a voice of comfort, but the quotation from Isaiah – 'In the wilderness prepare the way of the Lord' – comes from the passage that I read at that school carol service, from Isaiah 40, 'Comfort ye, comfort ye, my people, saith your God'. It is a voice telling good news, it is a voice of comfort but it also discomforts us as we hear of God's love for us and know that it requires a response from us, a turning to God that begins with repentance.

ARE YOU THE ONE WHO IS TO COME, OR ARE WE TO EXPECT SOME OTHER?

This is the question that John addresses to Jesus through his disciples. John was, as we have seen, the messenger, the forerunner, the sign to those who could read signs. The promised salvation was about to be accomplished. John was its herald. And yet so secret are the things of God that the herald did not know who it was who came after. He guessed that it was Jesus of Nazareth of whose teachings and miracles he had heard even in the prison into which Herod had cast him. And now he asks for confirmation. Perhaps he had already foreseen his death and, before he dies, he seeks assurance that the one he proclaimed is indeed come.

'Are you the one who is to come?' The question is cautiously phrased. When the doctrines of the faith are freely available, when there is no deep and hidden secret – or so it seems – there is no thirst for knowledge. John and his disciples want to know; they have a real desire for knowledge. In asking their question, however, they reveal little of their purposes. If Jesus had said, 'What are you talking about? I don't know what you mean', then they would have known that this was not the one and they would have looked for another. The answer Jesus gives is also for those who know already. He does not say simply, 'I am'. That would have been a statement that they could neither confirm nor deny. He points instead to that which can be heard and seen by all: the blind can see again, the lame are walking, lepers are cleansed, the deaf hear, the dead find new life, and the poor are hearing the good news. It is a curious collection that brings together the sick, the dead and the poor. Its very oddity may lead us to the conclusion that it has an inner or hidden meaning. Jesus was not just a wandering miracle-worker. He was the revelation of God and the bearer of salvation. It was not just kindness and compassion that impelled him to acts of healing; they only had meaning if they served the purpose of his becoming man.

John was not simply expecting a miracle-worker. The person whose impending arrival he proclaimed was to be far more complex than a mere worker of miracles. As John was the voice that cries in the wilderness, the clearer of paths, so the one he proclaimed was to be the fulfilment of prophecy. The darkness of sin was to be broken at last. The ray of light would penetrate the gloom. The upheaval caused by his coming would be like a new creation. Everything would be overturned, old certainties would fail, sin and death would prevail no more. So John asks, 'Are you he?'

Jesus, in reply, points to the disordered creation. People have eyes but they do not see; they have ears, but they do not hear; they have legs but they cannot walk. The poor bodies of lepers are disfigured and destroyed by disease. The very ones created in the image of the immortal God return to the dust of the earth. And the poor have no hope. This is not the will of God who saw that his creation was good and offered the gift of life. The disfigurement of the creation is only a symptom, however. It reveals how deep, how total the disorder is. The creation no longer fulfils the purposes of the Creator. Made in the image of God, man, male and female, is intended to be in a special relationship with God, a relationship called a covenant. The brokenness of the creation, revealed in sightless eyes, shows that that fundamental relationship is also broken.

'Are you the one who is to come?' The blindness that Jesus heals is that which will not see God or human estrangement from God:

a blindness that does not know sin when it sees it. The lameness is that of feet and legs that will not follow the way of the disciple, so that the lame sit despondent beside the way. The leprosy is the infestation of sin which deforms the soul and disfigures the divine image in humankind. The stopped ears of the deaf refuse to hear the message of the prophets calling for a return to the covenant, and death comes from that estrangement, from turning away from the giver of life. Among all there is a deep poverty of spirit. 'Are you the one?' asks John, and Jesus points to the spiritual dimension of his mission and not merely, as we might think, to the miraculous.

In the blind rush for material wealth, for status and advantage, a rush in which many today are trampled, the question that John asked is usually ignored. The answer is not heard. None are so blind, says the proverb, as those who will not see. Our age somehow seems blinder than others that have gone before. Every Advent I wonder whose coming will be celebrated on Christmas Day. Even Father Christmas is somehow less benevolent when he becomes a servant of greed and insatiable desire for possessions. In too many households the one who has come and is to come will be ignored. The body will be fed but not the spirit. And the real message of the Christmas for which these Advent reflections are a preparation is one that is stark in its austerity, rich in its promise, totally unsentimental, and unheard by many, perhaps by most. For the faithful, for those who see with the eye of faith, Christmas offers up its inner secret and gives us the deepest joy in knowing that here is the one who is to come and we need not look for another.

BEHOLD, THE LAMB OF GOD

The word 'lamb' – the Greek *amnos*, Latin *agnus* – appears only four times in the Gospels. Once each in Mark and Luke, when

the Passover lamb is mentioned, not at all in Matthew, and
twice in John, in the passage in which John the Baptist calls
Jesus the 'Lamb of God' – *agnus Dei*. It may seem a little
strange, therefore, that this designation of Jesus by John
becomes a really significant one, one that permeates the book
of the Revelation, which contains 29 references to the Lamb,
that penetrates the liturgy, and that, in addition to providing
one of the artistic attributes by which the Baptist is identified
in paintings, became a distinctive icon of Christ, crucified and
risen – the lamb and flag.

We can hardly hear the words 'Behold the Lamb of God that
takes away the sins of the world' without thinking of the
Eucharist, of the sacrificial victim laid upon the altar and
providing spiritual food for the faithful. As the choir takes up
the chant *Agnus Dei, qui tollis peccata mundi* (O Lamb of God,
that takest away the sins of the world) the priest at the altar
breaks the Body of Christ in preparation for communion. This
is a text especially associated with this breaking, known techni-
cally as the fraction. The chant at this point in the service was
probably introduced from the Christian East in the seventh
century, when Rome experienced a great influx of migrants
from the Greek lands, refugees from the invading power of
Islam. It is unusual among the prayers and hymns of the
liturgy because it addresses Christ himself directly. Nearly
every other prayer is addressed to God, making no distinction
of persons, or else is offered to the Father, through the Son, in
the power of the Holy Spirit. When at the Eucharist, however,
in the interval between consecration and communion, we rever-
ently address and humbly adore Christ made present under the
form of bread. We may be reminded of those short, powerful
hymns addressed to the Lamb upon the throne in the Revelation to John. We may also be reminded of G. H. Bourne's
popular hymn 'Lord, enthroned in heavenly splendour'. It has
a verse that links the eucharistic action not just to Calvary but

also to Bethlehem:

Though the lowliest form doth veil thee
As of old in Bethlehem,
Here as there thine angels hail thee,
Branch and flower of Jesse's Stem.
Alleluia! Alleluia!
We in worship join with them.

(*AMR*, 400)

All the rich biblical symbolism of the Lamb is evoked by this chant: the Passover lamb whose blood is put on the lintels and doorposts in Egypt; The Lamb that is our sacrifice and will become our food; The triumphant lamb upon the throne at the end of the world. And as from the heavenly Church the songs of thanksgiving sung by the elect resound to his praise, so the earthly Church, still engaged in life's pilgrimage, addresses its plea. Here too are evoked the presence of Christ, the crucified and risen Lord, making it impossible for us to celebrate Christmas without being aware of the shadow of the cross.

John's disciples seemed to be a little slow on the uptake. One day he calls Jesus 'the Lamb of God who takes away the sin of the world' and affirms that this is the one to whom he bears witness, the very Son of God, and his disciples do nothing about it. The next day he exclaims, 'Look! here is the Lamb of God!' This time the disciples follow Jesus. They are uncertain what it is they want of him, but he invites them to spend the day with him, and from this encounter, from sharing time with Jesus, they come to recognize that he truly is the Christ, the anointed one.

We too are invited to draw near with faith, to repent of our sins in accordance with the Baptist's preaching, to enter into communion with Jesus, to live our lives with him dwelling in us and we in him, as we receive his body and blood. The invitation to communion is an invitation to intimacy, an invitation to the supper and the marriage feast of the Lamb.

THE WORD AND THE VOICE

St Augustine of Hippo summed up the relationship between John the Baptist and Jesus by saying that John is a Voice, but the Lord is the Word. The Word exists in the beginning and is eternal; John is the Voice for a time. If the Word is taken away, the Voice has no purpose. Where there is no understanding, then what is uttered by a voice becomes just empty noise. A wordless voice beats on the air; it does not quicken the heart.

> *Now in this actual business of quickening the heart, let us observe the sequence of what happens. If I am thinking what to say, the word is already in my heart; but if I want to talk to you, I search for a way in which what is already in my heart may be also in yours.*
>
> *In this search for a way in which the thoughts of my heart may be conveyed to yours and lodge there, I use my voice, and with its aid I speak to you; the sound of my voice conveys the meaning of the word to you, and dies away, but the word that the sound has brought you has reached your heart without ever leaving mine.*

John the Voice made known the coming of the Word, but once the Voice has made itself heard, once it has performed its function, then it dies away. The Word remains lodged in our hearts.

Augustine notes that it can be difficult to distinguish word from voice. We can be stirred by a voice that carries little by way of content. In the Gospel, John himself was thought to be the Word. He knew himself to be only the Voice. He would not stand in the way of the Word and he responds to the questions put to him by saying, 'I am not the Christ, nor Elijah, nor the Prophet'. 'Who are you then?' he was asked. 'I am the voice of one crying in the wilderness: Prepare the way of the Lord (John 1.19–23)'. John is the Voice that breaks the silence and, calling men and women to repentance, prepares the way. John knew where salvation was to be found and pointed, in all humility, beyond himself to the one who was to come, the one greater than he would ever be.

GIVE ME THE HEAD OF JOHN THE BAPTIST

The Musée de Cluny in the Latin Quarter in Paris contains a remarkable collection of medieval objects, religious and secular, ranging from the painted mitres used in the Sainte-Chapelle to the tools of the kitchen. They were gathered together from the remnants left after first the Enlightenment and then the Revolution had shattered the old certainties and their monuments in church, monastery and palace. Though the collection is wonderful and wide ranging it is also oddly limited, limited that is by what survived, in the same way that our own national collections have to reach beyond the destructive force of the Reformation to uncover the Middle Ages.

Statues of the Blessed Virgin Mary abound and some are really delightful, especially those that show the Christ-child at the breast or else pulling at the neck of Mary's dress in order to be suckled. A little swinging cradle with bells that rang as it moved – a prop in a liturgical play – waited for the infant Saviour to be put in it. These devotional pieces are a source of endless delight. But there too is perhaps the most gruesome devotional piece I have ever come across – the severed head of John the Baptist on a plate. The head was life-size and the plate a good-sized platter. The martyred saint's eyes were unseeing, the eyeballs rolled back. His lips and teeth were parted and his tongue was visible. His whole face revealed the anguish caused by his imprisonment and summary decapitation. Quite how this object was used I do not know but it was so close to what the reality must have been that I read the

account of John's death given in Matthew and in Mark with both
devotion and horror. We have seen John already in the fulness of
life, thirty years old, tanned by wind and weather, declaring the
need for repentance and preparing for Christ's coming. We have
seen John as herald and messenger and will see him as the one who
baptizes Jesus in the Jordan, but we must also see him dead, his
noble head severed from his body because of the spite of Herodias
and the all too visible charms of Salome, as tradition calls the
dancing daughter, because of the foolish oath given by a drunken
king.

John Chrysostom, as quoted in *The Golden Legend*, said of him:

> *John is the school of virtues, the guide of life, the model of holiness, the*
> *norm of justice, the mirror of virginity, the stamp of modesty, the exemplar*
> *of chastity, the road of repentance, the pardon of sinners, the discipline of*
> *faith – John, greater than man, equal of angels, sum of the Law, sanction*
> *of the Gospel, voice of the apostles, silence of the prophets, lantern of the*
> *world, forerunner of the Judge, centre of the whole Trinity! And so great*
> *a one as this was given to an incestuous woman, betrayed to an adulteress,*
> *awarded to a dancing girl!*

There was no trial, no argument, no appeal, no reprieve. The oath
is made. The girl dances. The voice is silenced. John the Baptist,
the last of the prophets, the great forerunner of the morn, pays the
price for his commitment to truth. And when all was done, his
disciples came and took the body and buried it; and they went
and told Jesus.

5

O Come, O Come Emmanuel

'December hath xxxi Days' declares the Calendar of the Book of Common Prayer. Nicolas, Bishop, falls on the 6th, the Conception of V.M. (the Virgin Mary) on the 8th, Lucy, Virgin and Martyr on the 13th, and on the 16th 'O Sapientia'.

The various saints days, venerated with greater or lesser solemnity in different countries, mark the passage of Advent. According to tradition, Barbara, virgin and martyr, the daughter of a pagan from Nicomedia, was handed over to the authorities by her father when she converted to Christianity. She was one of the fourteen Auxiliary Saints, invoked for protection against thunderstorms and fire and the patron saint of artillerymen and firemen, of miners and horsemen. Her commemoration on 4 December was suppressed in 1969 but the day was and still is celebrated in German lands by cutting 'Barbara twigs' from fruit or nut trees. These were then kept in a warm place in the hope that they might bloom at Christmas. Perhaps this practice is related to the story that all the trees blossomed and bore fruit on the night that Jesus was born.

St Nicolas was celebrated on 6 December. Originally children left hay or straw for St Nicholas's horses. Later they put a shoe or boot out on the evening of 5 December, hoping to find it full of sweets, biscuits, nuts, etc. This is a well-known German rhyme addressed to him:

St. Nikolaus, leg' mir ein,	*St Nicholas, give me*
Was Dein guter Will' mag sein	*Whatever your good will may be;*
Äpfel, Nüss' und Mandelkern'	*Small children eating,*
Essen kleine Kinder gern.	*Apples, nuts and almonds.*

St Nicholas has a red gown, white beard, boots and sack. He also carries a stick and has a book of sins. He not only comes to reward good children but also to punish those who have been naughty. He sometimes has a frightening, dark companion who metes out punishment. He is named variously Ruprecht, Krampus, Pelzmärte, Klaubauf, Hans Muff, Butz, Buller or Pulterklas. In Southern Germany, Nicholas's companion is often a woman.

The great Advent festival day in Sweden is that of St Lucia, on 13 December, which is sometimes called Little Yule. A young girl dressed in white wears a crown of lighted candles on her head. She symbolizes the coming of light and prosperity to humans and animals alike. She visits the farms and homesteads in her area with gifts of food and drink. The Lucia Queen is accompanied by a long procession of young people carrying lighted candles and dressed as maids of honour or else as characters from the Bible or evil beings, trolls and demons. The practice of wearing the costume of devils or other evil beings is a part of the assumption that real devils can be scared away by those in 'devil disguises'.

Nothing in the Prayer Book explains what 'O Sapientia' means. I sat for many years as a schoolboy looking at the great seat occupied by the Chief Master of my school. Above his head it said 'Sapientia' and that was what his seat was always called. Unversed in Latin – still not one of my strengths – I was long unaware that it meant 'Wisdom'. And the calendar reference refers to the invocation of divine wisdom at beginning of a series of antiphons sung at Vespers in the last days of Advent.

THE O-ANTIPHONS

Antiphons are sentences, usually taken from Scripture, that are sung before and after the Psalms and Canticles (Benedictus at Lauds and Magnificat at Vespers) in the Divine Office. In Advent we find that the antiphons speak of the nature of the season in a way that collects and readings don't. They also contain some of the most wonderfully poetic and evocative lines to be found anywhere in the liturgy. The Roman Mass of Advent Sunday has no mention of the Nativity but the antiphons have. In the morning was sung

The Holy Spirit shall come upon you, O Mary:
fear not, you shall have in your womb the Son of God, alleluia.

and in the evening, before and after the Magnificat:

Fear not, Mary, for you have found grace with the Lord.
Behold, you shall conceive, and shall bring forth a son, alleluia!

Day by day the antiphons and responsories created a sense of antici- pation, and none more so than the great O-antiphons sung before and after the Magnificat in the latter part of Advent. In most of the Latin West they began with 'O Sapientia', on 17 December but in England they began on 16 December to accommodate an antiphon unique to the English liturgy, 'O virgo virginum'. These then are the O-antiphons (from the Roman Breviary):

O Sapientia, quae ex ore Altissimi prodisti, attingens a fine usque ad finem, fortiter suaviterque disponens omnia: veni ad docendum nos viam prudentiae.

O Wisdom, that proceeds out of the mouth of the Most High, reaching from end to end, mightily and sweetly disposing all things, come to teach us the way of prudence

O Adonai, et Dux domus Israel, qui Moysi in igne flammærubi apparuisti, et ei in Sina legem dedisti: veni ad redimendum nos in brachio extento.

O Adonai, and leader of the house of Israel, who appeared to Moses in the fire of the burning bush, and gave him the law on Sinai, come to redeem us by outstretched arm.

O radix Iesse, qui stas in signum populorum,

O root of Jesse, who stands as the ensign of

super quem continebunt reges os suum, quem gentes deprecabuntur: veni ad liberandum nos, iam noli tardare.

the peoples, before whom kings shall not open their mouths, to whom the nations shall pray, come to deliver us, tarry no more.

O clavis David, et sceptrum domus Israel; qui aperis, et nemo claudit; claudis, et nemo aperit: veni, et educ vinctum de domo carceris, sedentem in tenebris et umbra mortis.

O key of David, the sceptre of the house of Israel, who opens and no man shuts, who shuts and no man opens: come and lead the captive from prison, sitting in darkness, and in the shadow of death.

O Oriens, splendor lucis æterne, et sol iustitiæ: veni, et illumina sedentes in tenebris et umbra mortis.

O Orient, splendour of eternal light, and sun of justice, come and enlighten those who sit in darkness, and in the shadow of death.

O Rex gentium, et disideratus earum, lapisque angularis, qui facis utraque unum: veni, et salva hominem, quem de limo formasti.

O King of nations, and their desired one, and the corner-stone that makes both one, come and save mankind whom you formed out of dust.

O Emmanuel, Rex et legifer noster, exspectatio gentium, et Salvator earum: veni ad salvandum nos, Domine, Deus noster.

O Emmanuel, our King and lawgiver, the expectation and Saviour of the nations, come to save us, O Lord our God.

Each of the antiphons addresses Christ by one of his Old Testament titles or attributes. The first, 'O Sapientia', addresses him as the one who in the beginning made all things. The wisdom tradition in Jewish and Christian writings is too complex to explore here but in the apocryphal book of the Wisdom of Solomon wisdom is a feminine entity described as 'the fashioner of things' and as 'a breath of the power of God, and a pure emanation of the glory of the Almighty'. For in her, the writer continues,

> *there is a spirit that is intelligent, holy,*
> *unique, manifold, subtle,*
> *mobile, clear, unpolluted,*
> *distinct, invulnerable, loving the good,*
> *keen, irresistible, beneficent, humane,*
> *steadfast, sure, free from anxiety,*
> *all-powerful, overseeing all,*

and penetrating through all spirits
that are intelligent and pure and most subtle.

(Wisdom 7.22–23)

The Wisdom of God and the Word of God were seen to be one
and the same, and Pope Leo the Great writes in a letter that the
mystery of our reconciliation with God was to be fulfilled only
by the power of the Most High overshadowing Mary 'so that
within her spotless womb Wisdom might build itself a house and
the Word become flesh'.

Christ is then addressed in the second antiphon by the name of
God, *Adonai*, used in the Old Testament to replace the unspoken
divine name, the Tetragrammaton, rendered incorrectly as
'Jehovah' and by modern scholarship as 'Yahweh', the Lord. This
is he who appeared to Moses in the burning bush and gave the
Law on Sinai. Christ's incarnation is not, therefore, his first appear-
ance, but it differs from all previous ones. In the same letter, Pope
Leo the Great, exploring the reasons for the incarnation wrote:

No doubt the Son of God in his omnipotence could have taught and
sanctified men by appearing to them in a semblance of human form as
he did to the patriarchs and prophets, when for instance he engaged in a
wrestling contest [with Jacob] or entered into conversation with them,
or when he accepted their hospitality and even ate the food they set
before him [at Abraham's tent at Mamre].

The third antiphon would have a particular resonance for those
who were familiar with the Jesse tree in wall paintings and stained
glass. Jesse is at the root and above him are the many branches
leading either to Christ himself or to the Blessed Virgin Mary
holding the Christ-child enthroned on her lap. In between are
many of the kings and others whose names appear in the genealo-
gies, including the crowned figure of David, the psalmist of Israel,
recognizable from his harp. Jesse was, of course, David's father, of
whom Isaiah said, 'There shall come forth a shoot from the stump

of Jesse, and a branch shall grow out of his roots.' (Isaiah 11.1). And again, 'In that day the root of Jesse shall stand as an ensign to the peoples; him shall the nations seek, and his dwellings shall be glorious' (11.10).

Each of the antiphons describes the pitiable condition of the people whom God is urged to save: the Wisdom from on high is to teach the way of prudence; the Lord Adonai is urged to redeem his people with his outstretched arm; the root of Jesse is to set the people free; and the key of David and sceptre of the house of Israel is to bring the captive out of the darkness of prison and the shadow of death. The reference to David's key in 'O clavis David', the fourth antiphon, is again brought out from Isaiah, from chapter 22 where the prophet says, 'he shall open and none shall shut; and he shall shut and none shall open'.

The fifth antiphon, 'O Oriens', is entirely concerned with light in darkness. It is surely not accidental that it falls on 20 or 21 December. On the shortest day of the year in the northern hemisphere, the Church declares the splendour of the eternal light.

The penultimate antiphon is 'O Rex gentium'. Christ is not only called King here but also the one long desired and the cornerstone, *lapisque angularis*, who binds all things together. Come, pleads the text, come and rescue human beings, whom though didst make out of slime! That came to me as rather a surprise and could lead to a rather controversial rewriting of the funeral service with dust to dust replaced by slime to slime. The reference here seems to be to base material, to filth and to muddiness, and this fits – just – with the account on Genesis in which God made man from the earth, presumably shaping him out of mud or clay, before putting breath into him.

The last in the non-English cycle was 'O Emmanuel', a last call for Christ, Emmanuel, God with us, our King and lawgiver, to come and save us. It would have been sung at Vespers on 23 December. The next Vespers sung would have been that of Christmas with an antiphon of joyful expectation. Sung at evening, it looked forward to the sunrise on the feast of the Nativity:

Cum ortus fuerit sol de caelo, videbitis Regem regum procedentem a Patre, tamquam sponsum de thalamo suo.	*When the sun shall have risen in the heavens, you shall see the King of kings proceeding from the Father, as a bridegroom from his chamber.*

The English cycle was different. The vigil of the Nativity began at Vespers on 23 December and the Magnificat antiphon, though beginning with 'O', was addressed not to Christ but to his blessed Mother. Some say that this was because of England's great devotion to Mary.

O Virgo virginum quomodo fiet istud, quia nec primam similem visa es nec habere sequentem. Filie Jerusalem quid me admiramini divinum est mysterium hoc quod cernitis.	*O Virgin of Virgins, how shall this be? For neither before thee was any like thee, nor shall there be after. Daughter of Jerusalem, why marvel ye at me? The thing which ye behold is a divine mystery.*

COME, LORD, DO NOT DELAY

The origin of our services of lessons and carols is almost certainly to be found in the complex Roman liturgy of Ember Saturday, celebrated on the night before the Fourth Sunday of Advent. It was marked by very great solemnity and was certainly known to Edward White Benson, first Bishop of Truro and then Archbishop of Canterbury, who devised the sequence of nine lessons and carols for his cathedral long before it was adapted for King's College, Cambridge. The Ember Saturday liturgy was a night-time celebration and, as the Benedictine nun Aemiliana Löhr observed in her liturgical commentary, it retained 'the air of an age which was glad to watch a whole night through in God's praise'. The Mass was a very rich one. Löhr wrote of the depth and power presented in the rhythm of texts. All the texts, building on those already used on Ember Wednesday and Friday, speak of the coming of God, ritually expressing 'the primæval advent, the new birth, and the coming of Christ at the last day, advent in all the fullness of its developing meaning'. Certainly the key Advent words and themes appear: *adventus* in the Epistle, *veni* as the first word of the introit and in the third gradual and the tract, the coming of the bridegroom from his chamber and of the King to Sion. There is but one hint of the nativity – the mention in a collect of 'the approaching solemnity of your Son' – but the whole liturgy, permeated with Advent expectation, implores God to come and show his face.

The liturgy went on until Sunday morning and there was originally no separate provision for the Fourth Sunday of Advent – perhaps people were just too tired. The Sunday Mass set was put together from pieces of other Masses, shared a Gospel with the Saturday, and is a relatively late creation; it was given up entirely if the Sunday was Christmas Eve. The Ember Saturday Vigil said all there was to say about Advent. In Löhr's view, Advent could end there; the fourth Sunday adds nothing to it and merely binds together what has gone before. Pius Parsch in *The Church's Year of Grace* was of the same view:

> No new avenues remain to be explored in our preparation for Christmas during this fourth week of Advent, for the Church has unfolded her entire Advent message. She has led us to the threshold of Christmas with the joyous cry, 'Rejoice, for the Lord is near!', and more especially by the Ember Day observance. The liturgy has defined the picture of Christ the Saviour as clearly as it can for the time.

It began with a call for the Lord to come and to show his face. Isaiah 19.20–22, the first short lesson, told of how the Lord sent a saviour and defender to deliver Israel out of Egypt. The second lesson, Isaiah 35.1–7, is a promise that the desolate and impassable land will rejoice and flourish, bud forth and blossom; the dry land shall become a pool and the thirsty land springs of water. The third lesson, Isaiah 40.9–11, is familiar from our own Advent and Christmas carol-services, bringing good tidings to Sion, the city of God, and describing God as the shepherd who will feed his flock and gather the lamb in his arm, and take them to his bosom. The fourth lesson, and the last from Isaiah, chapter 45.1–8, does not at first sight belong among the familiar Advent readings from the prophet, for it is addressed not to Israel but to King Cyrus, called by God unexpectedly 'my anointed'. But God here shows that his power and favour is not limited to Israel and he uses Cyrus to subdue the nations. It concludes with an affirmation of God's power:

> *I am the Lord, and there is no other;*
> > *besides me there is no god.*
> *I arm you, though you do not know me,*
> *so that they may know, from the rising of the sun*
> > *and from the west, that there is no one besides me;*
> *I am the LORD, and there is no other.*
> > *I form light and create darkness,*
> > *I make weal and create woe;*
> > *I the LORD do all these things.*
>
> *Shower, O heavens, from above,*
> > *and let the skies rain down righteousness;*
> *let the earth open, that salvation may spring up,*
> > *and let it cause righteousness to sprout up also;*
> > *I the LORD have created it.*

(Isaiah 45.5–8 NRSV)

The last line is better known from the Advent prose 'Drop down dew, ye heavens, from above'; in Latin, *Rorate, cæli*.

The fifth lesson, Daniel 3.47–51, is the story of the fiery furnace and it leads into the singing of the Benedictus, the song of praise of the three young men, and a prayer that the flames of vice may not consume us! The Epistle, 2 Thessalonians 2.1–8, urges the believers to hope even though the forces of evil increase and the Gospel, Luke 3.1–6, brings us at the last to John's proclamation that the Kingdom of Heaven is at hand. One refrain was repeated many times in different ways throughout this long night of vigil, summed up in the words *Excita, Domine*: 'Stir up thy might, O Lord, and come to save us.'

6

Hail! Most Highly Favoured

The distance between creature and Creator can sometimes seem so great that communication must be impossible. God can seem to be 'out there', awesome in majesty, beyond imagination. Even Christ, truly God and truly human, could seem terrifying when seen as the one who comes again in power and great glory to judge the living and the dead. It was as a result of contemplating the nature of the divine majesty that one of the fundamental principles of Christian faith in the Middle Ages arose, that countless mediators move between us sinful mortals living out our time in this vale of tears and Almighty God, the Creator and sustainer of all that is. Opposed to this was one of the fundamental principles of the Reformation, that of there being only one Mediator between God and Man, Jesus Christ our Lord. The former view encourages a sense of the awful majesty of God, a sense of the Almighty dwelling in holiness so absolute, in light without shade, that convinces us of our unworthiness to approach him save by these mediators. The mediation works in two ways – as our prayers and supplications are conveyed to God by the saints, so too the grace of God is conveyed to us by way of relics, shrines, holy pictures, by miracles and evident acts of grace, and his wrath manifests itself in diverse diseases and sundry kinds of death. Chief among these mediators was the Mother of Mercy, the noble Queen of Heaven, the Lady of the world, the Mother and bride of the Everlasting King, the most blessed and perpetual Virgin Mary.

Reformation Christianity stripped her of her great feast day, 15 August, and removed from her this mediatorial role. It said that we must stand alone before God, having faith in Christ, relying only on divine grace, nourished by the Scriptures. Though it sought thereby to offer assurance that we would be saved, by grace, through faith, it retained the fear that sudden death would take us unprepared or that, because of the pains of death, we might yet fall from God. Remembering the tremendous respect given to Mary in England before the Reformation and the number of churches dedicated in her name, it is worth trying to find a middle way that honours Mary's unique role in the economy of salvation, that renders willing praise to her name, that welcomes her aid and that sees that she constantly points past herself to her beloved son, and who, especially at Christmas, presents her son for our worship and adoration. In doing this I am reminded of the question put by a Baptist to a Jesuit at an ecumenical study evening: 'What about Mary,' she said, 'she gets in the way.' And the Jesuit father replied: 'Does someone who prays for you get in the way?'

Devotion needs words. The idea that we pray best silently in the 'thinking position' – head cradled by a hand – is erroneous. We pray best standing or kneeling or prostrate. We pray best when we attend to or utter well-crafted words, phrases hallowed by use, refined by being constantly prayed. When we find that we have lost our own words for praying, when we find ourselves on our knees with nothing to say, we should, in the best tradition of Anglicanism, reach for a prayer book or else settle at the desk to write a prayer that expresses what we need to say, and then, thus tutored, say it. Prayers shape our faith and shape our devotion. From prayers we know that all hearts are open to God, that he hates nothing he has made, that he has caused all holy Scriptures to be written for our learning, and that he is the strength of all who put their trust in him. So what do we learn of Mary from the prayers addressed to her? She is called 'gracious Mother', glorious and holy Virgin, Queen of the heavens, Lady of all the angels. Bernard of Clairvaux, if he was indeed the writer of the *Memorare*, calls her the 'most loving Virgin Mary' and recalls that it is a thing unheard of that anyone ever had recourse to her protection, implored her help, sought her intercession, and was left forsaken. Certainly these sentiments fit well with the *Salve Regina*, one of the oldest of the Marian anthems, sung at the conclusion of Vespers or Compline for half the year. It dates from the end of the eleventh century and was perhaps completed by Bernard. Mary is hailed as Queen, Mother of mercy, our life, our sweetness and our hope. And the concluding line, set to one of the most beautiful pieces of plainsong, remains with anyone who hears it – O clement, O loving, O sweet Virgin Mary? The Advent and Christmas anthem calls her the gracious Mother of our Redeemer. Here is a language we do not often use in our religious observance. Here is a language we need to learn to use. It is a tender devotional language. It is a language of the heart rather than of the intellect, uniting us in love with the Mother of Christ as mother of the Church and mother of Christians. It is more often found in Christmas carols and poems than in modern liturgy.

MARY IN THE GOLDEN LEGEND

Jacobus da Voragine, the Dominican compiler of the *Golden Legend*, gives us a full account of the complex tradition concerning Mary's life before her appearance in the Gospels. He draws on a number of older works in order to do this and his account shows how there has always been a tendency to embellish and expand the biblical stories, to map the relations between biblical characters and to provide new ones where necessary. If you read these accounts you begin to think that everyone who appears in the Gospels was related to everyone else and it can begin to seem a little too cosy. But in the world of villages and small towns everyone really did know everyone else and their business, and nearly everyone was related to everyone else. The medievals wanted the biblical world to be like their world. Used to people living far from their place of birth and living increasingly solitary and independent lives, we find the effort to relate everyone rather contrived and unreal.

The basic account shows that Mary was a descendant of the house of David. Her parents, Joachim and Anna, are depicted as a righteous couple but childless after many years of marriage. They therefore make a vow to the Lord that any child they have will be given to the Lord. Joachim goes to Jerusalem for a festival but is reproached by the priest when he tries to bring his offering to the altar because, having no offspring, he has added nothing to God's chosen people and so cannot stand with those who have begotten sons. Feeling shamed and not wishing to suffer the scorn of his kinsmen, Joachim does not go home to Anna, but goes to stay with his shepherds in the fields. There an angel appears to him, tells him that he is wrongly reproached and promises that Anna will conceive. The angel then offers a short sermon on why God closes the womb, not as a punishment but so that when he grants the gift of a child it shall be seen to be the product of divine generosity and not of carnal desire. The angel provides a list of such miraculous births. Mary, he tells Joachim, will be filled with the Holy Spirit in the womb. Guided by the angel, Joachim returns to Jerusalem and, as foretold, meets the weeping Anna at the Golden Gate. They return home praising God and Anna conceives and gives birth to Mary.

At three years of age Mary goes to live in the Temple compound with other virgins and she stays there until, at the age of fourteen, the others return to their homes in order to marry. Mary says that she is unable to do this because she is vowed to the Lord. The High Priest hears a voice coming out of the Holy of Holies saying that all unmarried but marriageable descendants of David are to bring a branch to the altar. One such branch will bloom, a dove from heaven will descend upon it, and the man in question is the chosen husband of Mary. The order is duly given, yet when the men come to the altar with their branches none of them blooms. The High Priest therefore consults the Lord again. Joseph, who is an old man, has not gone up because he thought it inappropriate that he should have such a young bride. He is now commanded to bring his branch and it duly blooms and the dove appears and perches on it. After the espousals have been completed, Joseph returns to Bethlehem to prepare his house for Mary's arrival and to arrange the wedding, and Mary returns to her parents' home to await Joseph's summons. It is while she is in Nazareth that Gabriel brings his message to her.

GABRIEL TO MARY CAME

When I was a country parson in north Hertfordshire some fifteen years ago, serving the villages of Weston and Ardeley, I met a lady who lived just beyond the parish boundary on the back road to nearby Stevenage, at the house that had been E. M. Forster's *Howard's End*. Her name was Elizabeth Poston and though I much enjoyed meeting her I did not, alas, at that point know who she was. I remain grateful for that chance or providential meeting. Her *Penguin Book of Christmas Carols* is open in front of me as I write and it contains some of her lovely translations and arrangements of carols. One of the greatest of them and one of my favourites in *Angelus ad virginem*, 'Gabriel to Mary came'. It was, she explains, a fourteenth century Advent hymn, the tune in dance measure, and one of the greatest European songs. It is mentioned by Chaucer in *The Miller's Tale* where it was sung in the evening by Nicholas, the Clerk of Oxenford, to the accompaniment of his 'gay sautyre'

> *On which he made a nightes melodye*
> *So swetely, that all the chambre rong;*
> *And Angelus ad virginem he song.*

This was what he sang, together with Elizabeth Poston's translation:

Angelus ad virginem	Gabriel to Mary came,
Subintrans in conclave,	A gentle message bare he;
Virginis formidinem	deep in awe the Maiden bowed
Demulcens, inquit 'Ave!	To hear him say 'Hail, Mary'
Ave regina virginum;	There, heav'n and earth received his call,
Coeli terraeque Dominum	'Hail, hail thou queen of virgins all;
Concipies	Thou, yet undefiled
Et paries	Shalt bear a child
Intacta	Of sov'reign grace,
Salutem hominem;	To comfort all mankind;
Tu porta coeli facta,	Thou shalt bear him, Lord and God of all,
Medela criminum.'	To save our human race.'

(*Penguin Book of Christmas Carols*, 1)

The song itself is almost liturgical in the terseness of its language. Its simplicity contrasts with the complex relationships that circle Mary in the tradition. The stories of her birth, childhood and betrothal are too full of supernatural intervention and detract from the power of this encounter between the humble maiden and the angel. The Bible does not describe Gabriel and only says of the cherubim and seraphim that they have wings, but I still love the image of Gabriel conjured up by another carol – 'His wings of drifted snow, his eyes of flame'.

An angel is a messenger, another means by which the Word is given voice. It is no more than a messenger, though there is a tradition deeply imbedded in Scripture that an angelic fall precedes the fall of Adam and Eve. The medievals were fascinated by non-humans of all sorts and their world was peopled by fantastic and often grotesque beings. It was, however, no stranger than my elder son's world populated by figures from *Star Trek* and *Star Wars*, or my own childhood world of Daleks and Cybermen. But angels in particular gave medieval thinkers the opportunity to consider the diversity of the creation and the possibility that there were beings that had bodies but took up no space. When they debated the number of angels that could be got on a pin head, it was this idea of mass and corporeality that concerned them. Scripture testified, after all, to subtle bodies, like the post-resurrection body of Christ, that could pass through walls and yet sit on chairs, eat food and make a fire. If Scripture did not tell us more about angels than we read in Genesis and Revelation, together with the often painted story of Tobias and the angel, and the various appearances in the Gospels and Acts, then it was because such information was not required for our salvation. The first identified angel, however, was the fallen one, the ancient serpent, called also the Devil or Lucifer. The relation between the angel/serpent and Eve was paralleled by that between the angel/messenger and Mary. Saint Irenaeus wrote:

For just as the one [Eve] was seduced by the word of an angel so that she fled from God by disobeying his word: so the other, through the word of an angel, was brought good tidings, so that she received God by obeying his word. And just as the one was seduced into disobedience to God, so the other was persuaded into obedience to God. Thus the Virgin Mary came to be the advocate for the virgin Eve.

Gabriel is the messenger of God who brings a gentle message and tries not to terrify the over-awed maiden. Painting after painting shows Gabriel in God-given glory, a burning flame above his haloed brow, and wings of multi-coloured feathers, but with a gentleness of posture and expression that does not detract from the seriousness of his purpose. Mary often sits within, at prayer or reading, and Gabriel comes from without, through loggia or window, and above God the Father watches, the Holy Spirit over-shadows, and sometimes a tiny, tiny baby moves along a ray of light destined for the Virgin's womb.

THE WHOLE WORLD WAITS

More than any other writer or preacher, perhaps, St Bernard of Clairvaux explored Mary's humanity. His homily on the Annunciation in the collection of his sermons in praise of the Virgin Mother goes deeper into her feelings as she receives the angelic salutation, but also shows what rested on her reply. The angel waits, Bernard says, addressing Mary, waits for your reply 'for he wants to carry it back without delay to the God who sent him.' We, too, wait, Bernard continues, because a sentence of condemnation is laid on us and we await the words of mercy from the blessed Lady: 'For in your hands lies the hope of our salvation, and your consent will obtain our immediate release. The eternal Word of God made us, and see how we are dead men! But a word from you will see us re-made and brought back to life again.' Bernard joins Gabriel in trying to persuade Mary, who has not yet given an answer of any sort, that she should give free consent. Adam, weeping over his banishment, waits, he says; so do Abraham and David and the rest of the holy fathers, dwelling in the land of the shadow of death. The whole world waits because 'upon your word hangs the hope of comfort for us wretched creatures, of our ransom from captivity, our reprieve after sentence; in a word, the hope of salvation for every child of Adam, every member of your own race.' 'O Mary, do be quick and let us have your answer!' Bernard continues, impatiently.

Why do you delay? What have you to fear? Believe, praise, and accept what the Lord has told you. Temper your humility with a little boldness, your feeling of inadequacy with trust. There never was a moment when virginal innocence was so urgently called upon to cast discretion to the winds. No need for you, wise Virgin, to fear presumption in a matter such as this, for though your reticence reveals a becoming modesty, your love of us requires that silence should give place to speech.

And at last the Virgin's word is given: 'I am the handmaid of the Lord; let what you have said be done to me.'

MARY IN THE ADVENT LITURGY

To conclude our thinking about Mary we must return to the Roman liturgy. As I noted earlier, the place of Mary in the Advent and Christmas liturgy is not so immediately apparent as it is in popular devotion and in art. In general Mary belongs to the liturgical evening and to the Office rather than to the morning and to the Mass and in fullest form she belongs to the weekday not the Sunday. The Roman Stational Mass on the first Sunday of Advent was at St Mary Major, where the relics of Christ's crib are venerated in a replica of the grotto at Bethlehem. Since the fourth century it has had this particular association with the Nativity and was often called *S. Maria in praesepe* (in the stable). The stational Mass of Christmas Eve, and the first and third Masses of Christmas Day were celebrated here. The stational church can itself give a flavour to the liturgy; here it may be sufficient that Advent begins in this church.

The Roman Mass for Advent Sunday has no specific mention of the Nativity but the Magnificat antiphon at Vespers – *Ne timeas, Maria* – has the angelic salutation:

Fear not, Mary, for thou hast found grace
with the Lord: behold, thou shalt conceive,
and shalt bring forth a son, alleluia.

Vespers on the third Sunday also has a Magnificat antiphon concerned with Mary – *Beata es, Maria.*

Blessed art thou, Mary, for thou hast believed the Lord;
those things shall be accomplished in thee
which were spoken to thee by the Lord, alleluia.

The major statement of the Marian theme comes not in the Sunday liturgy but in that of the Ember Days, the Wednesday, Friday and Saturday after the Third Sunday of Advent. These are one of the *Quattuor Tempora*, the fasts occurring in each of the four seasons, which originated in the city of Rome and gradually spread from there across the Latin Church. Their origin is obscure and traditionally attributed to Pope Callixtus. Pius Parsch describes them as occasions of thanksgiving for the three great harvests of wheat, grapes and olives. The Ember Week ended with ordinations on the Saturday. *The Golden Legend* deals with them entirely in terms of reasons for fasting – e.g. we fast in winter 'to overcome the coldness of malice and lack of faith' – but their more ancient form of liturgy provided an opportunity for some significant preaching, notably by Pope Leo the Great and by Bernard of Clairvaux. The December days have a pronounced Advent character, though Wednesday and Friday are concerned with Mary and Saturday with the fullest possible expression of the Advent themes. This is not their original character and represents the combining of the existing Ember Day observance with the introduction of Advent.

The station on the Wednesday was again at St Mary Major. The introit was *Rorate, caeli*: 'Drop down dew, ye heavens, from above ... let the earth be opened and bud forth a Saviour.' The Mass had both an Old Testament lesson, from Isaiah 2, and a passage from Isaiah 7, with the prophecy 'Ecce Virgo concipiet' ('Behold, a virgin will conceive') in place of the Epistle. The Gospel was of the Annunciation. The *Ecce Virgo* was repeated at Communion. This Mass – known as the *Missa Aurea* – was apparently 'particularly esteemed by the faithful as a means of honouring our Lady in this mystery [the Annunciation] which is a preparation for the birth of our Saviour.' It was a Mass that caught the popular imagination. Though generally treated as a solemn votive Mass, using the collect of the Annunciation, and celebrated in white vestments, the official ruling was that it was a popular devotion. It clearly caused liturgical legislators some trouble and they grudgingly allowed that by custom and because of the devotion of the people it could be sung daily during the Novena before Christmas and the custom of singing it every day of Advent could be tolerated where it already existed. The geographical focus of this devotion was the *Alpenland* and Bavaria. Cardinal Joseph Ratzinger in *Dogma and Preaching* observed in an 'Advent sermon 'Among us Germans the Gospel of the Annunciation to Mary and the miraculous conception of the Son of God is read daily in the Rorate Masses'. It was also known in Germany as *Engelamt*, the angels' office. The *Missa Aurea* celebrated daily changed the whole tone of Advent and oriented it much more directly towards Christmas.

This involves the sort of tussle that we know so well today. One set of forces wants to keep Advent *as Advent* and Christmas *as Christmas* but those forces are countered by those that move the Christmas themes earlier and earlier in the season. The struggle – be it between official liturgy and popular devotion or between religious and commercial influences – has generally been fruitful and much of the richness of the celebration derives from it, but it can be destructive. One thing is clear, however, no matter what the compilers of official liturgy may do, devotion to the Virgin Mary breaks through and declares her to be, in the words of the final antiphon sung after Compline, the sweet Mother of the Redeemer.

Alma Redemptoris Mater quæ pervia cæli
Porta manes, et stella maris, succurre cadenti,
Surgere qui curat, populo: tu quæ genuisti,
Natura mirante, tuum sanctum Genitorem,
Virgo prius ac posterius, Gabrielis ab ore
Sumens illud Ave, peccatorum miserere.

Gracious Mother of our Redeemer, for ever abiding Heaven's gateway and star of the sea, succour the people, who though falling, striv to rise again.
Thou Maiden who bearest thy holy Creator, to the wonder of all nature;
Ever Virgin, after as before thou didst receiv that Ave from the mouth of Gabriel, have compassion on us sinners.

(*The Monastic Diurnal*

Part 2

Christmas

7

The Silent Night and the Word Incarnate

*While all things were in quiet silence
and the night was in the midst of her course,
your almighty Word, O Lord,
came down from your royal throne.*

This is the Magnificat antiphon of first Vespers of the Sunday within the Octave of Christmas. The same text is used for the beginning of the introit of the Mass of the Sunday after Christmas. It is a partial quotation from the book of Wisdom in the Apocrypha, the collection of 'hidden' books between the Old and New Testaments. It is not an easy text to translate but each of the versions I have looked at wants to quality the silence and to give it a quality because the text itself says *quietum silentium*, literally and tautologically 'quiet silence'. We know, however, that there are different types of silence. It is not the silence when no one speaks and we feel uncomfortable. It is not the silence of inactivity. It is a confident silence, a hopeful absence of sound, the being still in which we can know God. The difference here is like the difference between waiting as a child in the dentist's waiting-room and that attentive waiting that is characteristic of Advent. The Revised Standard Version of the Bible renders it like this: 'For while gentle silence enveloped all things, and night in its swift course was now half gone, thy all-powerful word leaped from heaven, from the royal throne' (18.14–15). The Jerusalem

Bible makes it a 'peaceful silence' and the Revised English Bible sees that 'all things were lying in peace and silence'.

A little linguistic detective work may be useful here. Wisdom was written in Greek but comes to the Western Church in Latin. The Greek text uses *logos* for 'word'. *Logos* comes into English in the -ology ending that we use to quality various sorts of study. It means talking about something. So theology may be defined as words or speech about God, as *theos* means God. *Logos* is the word St John uses at the beginning of his Gospel when he says 'In the beginning was the Word (*Logos*)'. In Latin, *logos* is rendered as *verbum*, from which we get verb and verbal. John's Gospel provides a crucial reading for Christmas. John 1.1–14 was the passage set as the Gospel for the Mass of the Day and as such it came over into the Prayer Book. It is also the ninth reading in the King's College, Cambridge, pattern of lessons and carols. The first verse says *In principio erat Verbum*, 'In the beginning was the Word'.

But in the antiphon and introit 'word' is given as *sermo* not *verbum*, which seems to be rather a curious choice. This is what the Vulgate, the Latin translation of the Bible uses. It would have been easier to follow John and use *verbum* but this other word may help us to understand what is going on when God becomes incarnate. In general use in medieval thought, in the writings of St Thomas Aquinas, for example, *verbum* means the second person of the Trinity as the Word of God and the *verbum essentiale, notiale* or *personale* signifies the essence of God. *Sermo* is rather different; it means not merely a word but a discourse, a conversation. We, of course, get the word 'sermon' from it. Here it shows us that the incarnation initiates a new and definitive phase in the discourse, the conversation, between the creation and the Creator. The echoing voices of Advent, culminating in the call for Christ to come among us, here find their reply.

The structure we have already looked at – speech, silence and response – is an essential part of Christmas. 'Silence' is a word applied to the night of the Nativity in many texts. It is the *Stille*

Nacht and the *heilige Nacht* long before Joseph Mohr used these words or Bishop Phillips Brooks told how silently the wondrous gift is given and Edmond Sears spoke of the world lying in solemn stillness. The medieval Cistercian preacher Guerric, Abbot of Igny, in his *Liturgical Sermons*, makes much of this in his fifth sermon for Christmas. He contrasts hearing the Word with seeing the Word, pointing out that God, knowing that human minds are incapable of perceiving invisible things, unwilling to be taught about the things of heaven, and slow to yield to faith without visible testimony, made his Word both visible and tangible.

> *Truly it is a trustworthy word and deserving of every welcome, your almighty Word, Lord, which in such deep silence made its way down from the Father's royal throne into the mangers of animals and meanwhile speaks to us better by its silence. Let him who has ears to hear, hear what this loving and mysterious silence of the eternal Word speaks to us.*

The human response is 'with joyous voice' to loudly sing 'the glory of their new-born King'. And that is what we often do on Christmas night. Leaving our dinner tables, our parties, our televisions and books, and the preparations for the next day's festive meals, we venture out in the dark and cold and make our way to church. Christmas night is different from any other night. We know nights of exhausted sleep, nights of work, nights of restless wakefulness, nights of joy, and nights marked by anxiety and grief. Christmas night is called a holy night, a still and silent night in which God draws near, in which God wills to be found.

God sometimes seems not to want to be found. God can seem distant, detached, departed, even dead. *Deus absconditus*, said our forebears in the faith, who were more certain in their dealings with the Deity, aware of divine absence as well as of divine presence. God, they said, had absconded, was absent, needing to be sought after, wanting to be looked for. In our experience the divine presence can be like the tide, only less predictable.

Sometimes it floods us, saturating our lives, marking us indelibly and forever, creating a sense of loss if and when God again withdraws or we somehow lose our ability to hear his word and to know his presence. In the absence of the flood, our spirits can become arid, dry and brittle, and we long for it to come again. The sense of presence and absence is attested to by the prophets, but recall that when Isaiah urges God to 'rend the heavens and come down' and to consider the lot of his people, God replies that he was ready to be sought by those who did not ask for him and to be found by those who did not seek him.

LET US GO EVEN UNTO BETHLEHEM

On Christmas night God undoubtedly wills to be found by the many and not only by the few. On Christmas night he would have us go to the little town of Bethlehem, to the Bethlehem of our hearts and our imaginations, to that inner place where God dwells. He would have us go with wonder and delight, as those who have seen angels. He would have us go willingly and with haste as he draws nears to us and wills to be found by us. And what will we see there? what scene will greet our eyes? A scene that is well known but is forever new.

We see a little babe. Those who have written of him, those who composed plays and poems and songs, found themselves compelled to use the sweetest endearments about him. This is the baby king, the sweet and dear one, comely and pure, a little flower. We know the scene so well because artists have delighted to depict it. We see the stable, the manger, the ox and the ass. Let us therefore find our place for a moment in the animal warmth of the stable and gaze at the child and at his Virgin Mother.

There is a tradition that the baby cried. We find it, among other places, in an old French carol 'Leaping and dancing' that comes from Roussillon, was collected by Joseph Canteloube and is included in Elizabeth Poston's book. A little after birth, a little after coming into the world he would redeem, the Son of God, cried out, for he was touched in that moment by the world's sin and grief, by the burden of labour and the inevitability of death. The babe cried, says the tradition, and his mother took him up and comforted him, singing:

> Hush, O hush, thou little one, hush;
> God has willed thou liest here thus.

But it is more than this, more than the will of God. This child is God the Word, come down from the royal throne. The paradox is stunning. The Creator of all things is born. The timeless one enters time. God empties himself and becomes man. No play-acting this. 'Robed in flesh the Godhead see' is wrong. God does not toy with us. This is the incarnate deity. The incarnation – the enfleshment of God – shows us how God works, and so tells us something of God's nature. We notice the hidden element. The Annunciation comes to Mary and to her alone, and she ponders in her heart the angel's message. Joseph too is a discreet person. God communicates by angelic messenger, by dreams, and by pointing to prophecy. We see God draw out the response of willing co-operation. There is no compulsion here. There is the need to venture in faith. We notice as well how God brings his Son into the world through poor and humble people and takes the risk of submerging him in human history, making him fully human, even as he is fully divine. We see the interaction between human and divine, not just in him, but in ourselves. We see heaven touch earth. That conjunction, that interaction makes Christmas night a most holy night.

God is enfleshed, become incarnate of the Virgin Mary his mother. And as we celebrate Christmas, he again draws near to us. Seeking, therefore, we find him – we find him in his house and in his sacraments, and among his people and in his word but also in our imaginations and in our hearts. And by this means we are

again drawn into God's promise and drawn into the moment
when heaven touches earth, when a babe is born and angels sing
to shepherds. We are drawn there to watch Mary rock the babe,
to soothe his cries and to hear her sing:

> *Hush, O hush, thou little one, hush;*
> *God has willed thou liest here thus.*

And to know, as the Creed affirms, that this is for us and for our
salvation.

O MARY, DID LOVE NEARLY
DESTROY YOU?

'The Nativity, at night' by Geertgen Tot Sint Jans is a religious
painting of great intensity. It was painted in Holland between
1480 and 1490 by a man largely unknown. His name indicates
that he lived with the Knights of St John of Jerusalem. He is said
to have died between 1485 and 1495, being only twenty-eight
years of age. He was one of a number of artists who took up a
theme from the writings of St Bridget of Sweden that recount her
vision of the birth of Christ. She wrote that 'the new-born child
radiated such ineffable light and splendour, that the sun was not
comparable to it, nor did the candle, that Saint Joseph put there,
give any light at all, the divine light totally annihilating the
earthly light of the candle.'

   Lying naked in the manger, not yet wrapped in swaddling
bands, the babe of Bethlehem truly radiates light in Geertgen's
picture. He lights up Mary's face. She has about her a look of awe
and wonder, a look of love and fear, because of this baby
entrusted to her. Round his head the angels have gathered and
they reflect the babe's light. Their fingertips touch as they stand,
like Mary, in an attitude of prayerful adoration. One has hands

apart and a look of joyous amazement. Less brightly illuminated are the ox and the ass, and Joseph, standing in the shadows. In the distance we can see another bright angelic form addressing the shepherds, standing by their fire, on the hillside. The flames of the fire are dim compared to the angelic brilliance.

What was Mary thinking? What did she ponder in her heart as the events of the first Christmas unfolded? The Franciscan poet Jacopone da Todi, who lived in the thirteenth century, captured in one of his Lauds, addressed to the Virgin, exactly those feelings that Geertgen put on Mary's face two hundred years later:

> *O Mary, what did you feel when you first saw Him?*
> *Did love nearly destroy you*
> *As you gazed upon Him, how could you sustain such love?*
> *When you gave Him suck, how could you bear such excess of joy?*
> *When he turned to you and called you Mother*
> *How could you bear being called the Mother of God?*
> *O Lady I am struck mute*
> *When I think of how you looked on Him,*
> *As you fondled him and ministered to His needs.*
> *What did you feel then*
> *When you held Him at your breast?*
> *The love that bound you makes me weep!*

(*AMR*, 118)

8

The Song of the Angels

One of the hardest Sundays on which to preach is the Sunday after Christmas when it falls on the 29th or later. It always feels like clearing up after a party – there are a lot of remains but they are fragmentary and disconnected. The babe sleeps in the manger but the shepherds have gone and gentle Mary has settled into some routine of feeding and changing him. Joseph, meanwhile, attempts to procure food and to find a different and better place to lodge. What are these fragments and remains? There is the prophetic word that is still obscure even when interpreted, there is the angelic message, the Virgin Mother, the heavenly host and the frightened shepherds, and of it all we ask the morning-after question 'what does it mean?'

Put simply, with risk of over simplification, this birth brings God among us in a unique and special way. It may be enough to say that the babe of Bethlehem is God with us and God for us, but the human mind strives to know more, not least because the words 'God' and 'man' belong in two different classes and we want to know how they can be brought together. It is a paradox, an apparent contradiction, a great and mighty wonder. The office of Christmas night includes this responsory:

O magnum mysterium et admirabile sacramentum, ut animalia viderent Dominum natum, jacentem in præsepio. Beata Virgo, cujus viscera meruerunt portare Dominum

O great mystery and wonderful sacrament, that animals should see the new-born Lord lying in a manger. Blessed is that Virgin, whose womb deserved to bear Christ our

Christum. Ave, Maria, gratia plena; Dominus tecum.

Lord. Hail Mary, full of grace, the Lord is with thee.

We find ourselves faced by the twofold tendency that is found in so much of our Christian living – to worship and to understand. At the stable, as at the altar, I want to worship. I want to be brought to my knees, lost in wonder, love and praise. But when I open my mouth to express my worship, to give voice to my adoration, I need words and words, as we now know well, are the vehicles of meaning. To satisfy my need to adore, my words must be expressive of what I behold. They must also make sense. How can our adoration of the Word, the divine Logos, be irrational, incoherent or nonsensical? But think of other occasions when we struggle for words; think of being in love. The language of love is chosen more for its poetic, evocative quality than for its accuracy but it cannot be entirely devoid of a relation to our daily converse, domestic or business, literary, artistic or educational. To this end we have often found it easier to borrow our language, to use what the tradition has employed, the words of prayers and carols. A few Christmases ago, in *The Roads from Bethlehem*, I found just such a language in an old play, the so-called Second Shepherd's Play, where one of the shepherds addresses the Christ-child:

> *Hail, sovereign Saviour, for you have us sought!*
> *Hail, noble child and flower, that all things has wrought!*
> *Hail, full of favour, that made all of nought!*
> *Hail! I kneel and I cower. A bird have I brought*
> *To the child.*
> *Hail, little tiny moppet!*
> *Of our creed you are the head;*
> *I would drink of your cup,*
> *Little day-star.*

Rough and ready theology, of course, but absolutely right as we see a 'little tiny moppet' who is also a 'darling dear, full of Godhead'. The Word that was in the beginning and from the beginning is incarnate, enfleshed, born of a woman, a helpless baby lying in a manger. In the beginning was the Word and now that same Word, through whom all things were made, is made flesh and becomes man, for us and for our salvation. This is a great mystery, the *magnum mysterium* of the responsory.

MYSTERY AND SACRAMENT

In biblical and theological terms, a mystery is not something hidden that will be revealed, nor something presently mysterious that will become clear. Rather, mystery is always present when the creature encounters the essential nature of the Creator. The one who creates is always, in his essence, incomprehensible to those he has created. At such points of encounter the eye of faith is needed. Faith befriends the outward sense and so makes the inner vision clear. The incarnation, the enfleshment of the second person of the holy and undivided Trinity is just such a moment. Without the informing principle of faith a baby in a manger is just that, a baby lying rather incongruously in a manger. The responsory speaks not only of a great mystery but also of *admirabile sacramentum*, a wonderful sacrament.

Now a sacrament may be simply defined as an outward and visible sign of inward and spiritual grace, that is to say as the visible indication of invisible grace. The outward sign is clear enough in the sacraments given by Christ to the Church – the baptismal washing, the anointings, the bread and wine of the Eucharist, the laying-on of hands. These are sacraments in a proper sense, but clustered around them is a larger group of signs that take their origin from Christ, the effective sign of God's presence. The sign becomes a sacrament when it is seen by the eye of faith. As St Thomas Aquinas says of the Eucharist, 'faith our outward sense befriending makes the inner vision clear'. Faith is needed if the visitors to the stable are not just to see a baby, ordinary and commonplace, lying unexpectedly in a manger.

It is precisely this incongruity, this unexpectedness, that struck the writer of the responsory. It is a great mystery that animals should see the new-born Lord in a manager. This attracts his attention more than the coming of the shepherds. Scripture says nothing of the animals but the tradition has, wisely, found a place for the ox and the ass, and story and legend have found a place for the robin, the spider, and even the beetle. All created beings acknowledge the presence of the Lord of glory. The ox and the ass, according to the *Golden Legend*, miraculously recognized the Lord and went down on their knees to worship him. This too was counted as a sign and a fulfilment of Isaiah's prophecy (1.3): 'The ox knows its owner and the ass its master's crib.'

WHOM HAVE YOU SEEN, O SHEPHERDS?

Whom have you seen, O shepherds?
Speak and tell us, who has appeared on earth?
'We saw the new-born Child and choirs of angels, loudly praising the Lord.'
Speak, what have you seen? And tell us of the birth of Christ.
'We saw the new-born Child and choirs of angels, loudly praising the Lord.'

(Roman Breviary, 1st Nocturn of Christmas Day)

This is a responsory from the Christmas liturgy, involving a dialogue between cantor and choir. From this dialogue, and from a similar one that interrogates the women at the tomb on Easter Day, liturgical drama and medieval theatre began. The dialogue is wonderful in its simplicity, evoking the straightforward world of the shepherds. We see them in many paintings of the Nativity coming piping to the stable, waking the baby, rough and red-faced.

At Midnight Mass in Llandaff Cathedral, Christmas 1978 – my last such service before my ordination to the Diaconate – the Dean, Alun Davies, asked why the message came to the shepherds in the fields. He asked us to imagine the gathering in Bethlehem, the crowded city, the families who had come to be registered, relatives close and distant. He bade us think of the endless talk, the exchange of news, the telling of life stories by those who had not seen each other for years, and, along with the talk, the flowing wine and the merry-making. Perhaps Bethlehem was not at that moment a place of stillness and silence and in the noise the angelic voices might have gone unheard. So the messengers went out into the crisp night, out into darkness and silence, to address those who would hear.

Another possibility is that here again God chooses those who are on the margins, whose word does not count, just like the women at the tomb, who cannot be witnesses in court. Shepherds were marginal. They lived among the sheep. They were prone to drinking excessive amounts of alcohol in order to pass those long nights of watching the sheep, taking turns to sleep, always fearful of the wild animals. As the incarnation became a reality, God was already exalting the humble and meek. The shepherds would not understand. They would repeat the angelic proclamation of the birth of Christ the Lord, but might too easily be dismissed with a tapping of the head because it was easy to go crazy in the fields night after night. Another principle is here enunciated – those who have ears, let them hear. For those who looked for the consolation of Israel there were signs enough. Shepherds might not understand but they knew something wonderful had happened and they returned from Bethlehem glorifying and (praising God. It was on that return journey that the question in the responsory was put to them: '*Quem vidistis pastores?*' 'What have you seen, O shepherds?' 'We saw the new-born Child and choirs of angels, loudly praising the Lord.'

SING WE YULE TILL CANDLEMAS

When the shepherds have returned to their flocks and the angels to heaven, the liturgical cycle moves swiftly – and strangely – on. The anonymous fifteenth-century carol, 'Make we mirth' calls for jubilation throughout the Christmas season right up to the presentation of Christ in the Temple on 2 February. It is a sort of sacred equivalent of the Twelve Days of Christmas.

> *Make we mirth*
> *For Christ's birth,*
> *And sing we Yule till Candlemas.*

It begins with the first day of the Yule season and the birth of Jesus, before it turns to the three days after Christmas and their odd assortment of saints.

> *The second day we sing of Stephen*
> *That stoned was and ascended even*
> *To God, who saw him stoned from heaven,*
> *And crowned was for his prowess.*

The third day is that of St John, Apostle and Evangelist.

> *The third day belongs to Saint John,*
> *Who was Christ's darling, dearer none,*
> *To whom he gave when he should be gone*
> *His mother dear for her innocence.*

The fourth day of Christmas belongs to the Holy Innocents.

> *The fourth day of the children young*
> *That Herod had put to death with wrong,*
> *And Christ they could not tell with tongue*
> *But with their blood bore him witness.*

Our poet does not offer a verse for every day, but notes the principal commemorations – after the Innocents comes Thomas Becket on the fifth day, the naming of Jesus and his circumcision on the eighth day, the coming of the Magi on the twelfth day and the purification of the Virgin and the presentation on the fortieth day.

The combination of feasts may seem strange. Why should we leap from the birth of Christ to the first martyr, then to the Beloved Disciple, then the Innocents, slain after the coming of the Kings? The answer comes in part from the history of the Church's year. The observance of the Nativity is a later addition to the liturgical cycle. The first features were the celebration of the death and resurrection of Christ and the days of the martyrs. So Stephen would have been there first. And then John. After that Christmas, commemorating the whole incarnation and then the Innocents. The Epiphany is not originally a commemoration of the Magi but of the revelation of God in Christ, to the Magi, at his baptism in Jordan, and at Cana's wedding feast.

But the liturgical year is, in parts, like an old building acquired by a new owner who is not responsible for the original building or for the series of additions, extensions and remodelling that have subsequently taken place. The new owner may make some alterations but the original shape is still visible. And more than that, the new owner sees the building as a whole unaware, to some extent, of the history, and so sets out to justify what is to be found there. This, I must say, makes for something that is idiosyncratic but fascinating – like a pocketful of coins in my childhood, with heads of monarchs from Victoria to Elizabeth II, and values drawn from diverse systems, as shillings, pennies, florins, and half-crowns mingled together.

So there have been attempts to justify the relation between St Stephen and St John and the birth of Christ. Stephen is seen as the first witness to the reality that John proclaims – the Word being made flesh. John provides a theological commentary on the story told by Luke and Matthew, and – as our poet declared – the beloved disciple also has a special relation to the beloved Mother. With these two our celebration of the Nativity continues but it also expands beyond the manger and the stable and is placed in a broader context, helping us to understand how God became incarnate.

9

Festive Laughter and the Cry of the Innocents

Before Christmas 1360 Bishop John Grandisson of Exeter wrote to the clergy of his cathedral and of other collegiate churches in his diocese. He said this:

> It has come to our knowledge, not without grievous amazement and displeasure of heart that for these past years and some years preceding, at the most holy solemnities of Christ's Nativity, and the feasts of St Stephen, St John the Apostle and Evangelist, and the Innocents, when all faithful Christians are bound to busy themselves the more devoutly and quietly in praise of God and in Church Services, certain Ministers of our aforesaid Church, together with the boys, not only at Matins and Vespers and other hours, but also (which is more detestable) during the solemnity of the Mass have rashly presumed, puffing the fear of God behind them, after the pernicious example of certain Churches, to associate together within the Church itself and play certain foolish and noxious games, unbecoming to clerical honesty.

(Coulton, Life in the Middle Ages)

It was not the first time he had addressed his clergy in this way. In October 1330 he complained that 'certain Vicars and other Ministers of our Cathedral Church ... fear not to exercise irreverently and damnably certain disorders, laughings, gigglings, and other breaches of discipline, during the solemn services of the church'. He gives a specific example: those who stand at the upper stalls in the cathedral choir and have lights within their reach at

Mattins, the night office of the Church, 'knowingly and purposely throw drippings or snuffings from the candles upon the heads of such as stand at the lower stalls'. And the Bishop knows what their purpose is: it is that of exciting laughter and perhaps of generating discord. Disorderly laughter and derisive gigglings are his target as he seeks to remove the mockery of divine worship which appears to have become the custom at this time. Evidence from a number of greater churches in England and France points to the Christmas period, and especially the Holy Innocents on 28 December and the Circumcision of Christ on 1 January, as the main time for this sort of behaviour.

We must, however, remember that the liturgy and offices in these churches went on for many hours and that human nature can only stand so much solemnity. The weak state of health caused by the long periods spent in quire, together with fasting and monastic silence, was recognized as a legitimate disorder. Monks who were afflicted by it moved among their fellows as if half dead and were unable to read or sing or perform the duties required of them. They were allowed to walk in the vineyard or the garden and beside the river so that by repose, recreation and diet they might regain their former state of health. Even when the liturgy was not of increased solemnity monks and canons had to be reminded not to make needless signs during services or needless conversation, or to cut their nails, write, smile, whittle, throw one foot across the other, stretch out their legs or sit with their legs wide apart. They should lower and raise their seats quietly and not be constantly looking around to see what is going on. Grandisson had also heard that when someone read a text incorrectly the clergy in the stalls would shout out, 'Cursed be he who told that last lie!'

The celebration of Christmas began with solemn vespers on Christmas Eve and then the Midnight Mass followed by Mattins and the other offices, with two further solemn Masses to be sung. Vespers of Christmas Day overlapped with first vespers of St

Stephen, St Stephen overlapped with St John, and St John with the Innocents, leading into the feast of St Thomas Becket. There were extra processions and extra observances to mark each feast but the liturgy also contained a form of release in the ceremonies associated with the boy-bishop. It was, perhaps, the abuse of these ceremonies which caused Bishop Grandisson to complain. To understand what was going on we must first look at the Holy Innocents themselves.

A VOICE WAS HEARD IN RAMAH

The story of the slaughtered infants of Bethlehem is part of the account in Matthew 2 of the birth of Jesus and the visit of the Magi. The narrative has four distinct but related parts. In the first, the Magi come to Jerusalem to enquire where the child was born and receive an answer from Herod. In the second, they deliver their gifts to the child. In the third, an angel appears to Joseph warning him that Herod is searching for the child to destroy him, and so he is to take the child and his mother and flee into Egypt. In the final section, Herod, infuriated that he has been tricked by the Magi, orders that all children in and around Bethlehem who are two years old or under are to be killed. The section concludes with the words of the prophet Jeremiah (31.15):

> *A voice was heard in Ramah,*
> *wailing and loud lamentation,*
> *Rachel weeping for her children;*
> *she refused to be consoled,*
> *because they are no more.*

The parts were early separated. The feast of the Epiphany became primarily a celebration of the Magi. The Gospel at the Epiphany Mass concluded with the words *reversi sunt in regionem suam*, 'they returned to their own land'. There is some evidence, notably a sermon of Pope Leo the Great, indicating that the Innocents were for a time included in the celebration of the Epiphany but in North Africa they were commemorated on 28 December from the fifth century and the Innocents were commemorated as martyrs. It may seem rather odd that we observe their commemoration nine days before the Epiphany, but this is the result of the complex development of this part of the liturgical calendar. It certainly gave medieval commentators pause for thought. The general view was that it took the Magi a year to reach Bethlehem and that, as Herod was called away to Rome thereafter, it was another year before he ordered the murder. By this means the commentators explained how the Magi could have seen the natal star and how the Holy Innocents come before the Epiphany.

The commemoration has clearly never been straightforward. The Mass, though it fell in the festive season after Christmas, was celebrated in violet or purple vestments, with dalmatic and tunicle, but without the *Gloria in excelsis*, Creed or Alleluia. That is to say, it had a penitential character, unless it was a Sunday, when it was celebrated in the red vestments used for the feasts of martyrs. 'The Church puts on the garments of mourning today,' said one liturgical writer. The practice is clearly ancient, dating from at least the ninth century. A number of arguments were given to explain the variations. First, though they were martyrs, the Innocents died before Christ and so descended into hell. Joyful chants were used if it was a Sunday because every Sunday was a day of resurrection and were also used on the octave day, a week after the commemoration, to recall that Christ descended into hell and raised them up. Some commentators found this argument unacceptable because of the festive nature of the commemoration of the beheading of John the Baptist who also died before Christ. Second, we are urged to grieve along with the mothers of these children, and third, the children could not be called victorious because, though innocent and unstained, they had not fought for the faith.

Yet in practice the Holy Innocents, more than St Stephen and St John, belonged to the feast of the Nativity. St Augustine said that the hatred of Herod was more than balanced by the grace and blessing of God who brought them forth to eternal life. The responsories in the Office equated the Innocents with the 144,000 redeemed from the earth who were virgins, had not defiled themselves with women, and who reigned with God and the Lamb. The Mattins antiphons recount the story of Herod's rage and the slaughter of the children, but the responsories, as a sort of counterpoint, return constantly to the liturgy in heaven and the innocent beneath God's throne. Grandisson sees one aspect of the liturgy on this day – the ceremonies of the boy-bishop – as confirming that Christ is truly a child as well as the divine mediator, the great bridge builder.

THE BOY-BISHOP AND THE FEAST OF FOOLS

The children, especially the choristers and young clerks, were indulged on this day, and it must have been a great relief after the lengthy Christmas services. In many greater churches and colleges there was a boy-bishop, elected on St Nicholas's Day, who ruled the church and its close on the Innocents' Day. He wore full pontificals (that is, the vestments of a bishop or pontiff) including a mitre, ring and crosier or pastoral staff. All the other boys had to give him the reverence due to a bishop and he presided at all the ceremonies of the day except the Mass. He also preached sermons, written specially for him. The canons and older clergy took the place of the boys, carrying candles, books and censers, and the boys took the higher stalls as if they were canons. Sometimes the feast was extended over several days and included processions to other churches and to nunneries.

Sometimes the celebration of the Innocents must have declined into impious gigglings and tomfoolery but it is not to be confused with the New Year's revels called the Feast of Fools (*festum fatuorum* or *stultorum*) and more generally associated with the Circumcision. In this strangely inverted celebration 'bishops', 'archbishops' or 'popes' of Fools were chosen. They acted like the boy-bishops wearing mitres and carrying pastoral staffs and having crosses carried before them like archbishops on visitation. The attendant clergy wore masks and other disguises, often being made to look like the sort of monsters we see depicted at the gate of hell. They dressed as women or as minstrels or wore vestments inside out, wore wreaths of flowers and orange peel spectacles, and danced in the choir. The liturgy was parodied. Pudding and sausage, even old shoe-leather, were burnt in the thurible. They spoke and sang in high-pitched voices or howled or sang dissonantly. Again the lower clergy took the higher stalls in choir and much was made of the word in the Magnificat *deposuit*, the putting down of the mighty from their thrones.

The tragic death of the children of Bethlehem provided an opening for an indulgent attitude toward the children and it was not only they but everyone involved who enjoyed a period of misrule, of playful mockery and laughter. As the masks representing fantastic beasts and evil spirits were supposed, in the Advent visits, to scare away real evil spirits, so the vices were supposed to be put to flight by this short period of release from constraint. The medieval view, opposed by those who called for the suppression of all such festivities, was that it was really not very serious but a way in which the foolishness innate in us all could abound once in a year and then evaporate. The feasts were alikened to the air holes that prevented wine bags and casks from exploding. For a whole year the clergy devote themselves to the service of God; once a year they need the release of games and foolishness and so that afterwards they might return more strongly to wisdom.

Part 3

Epiphany and Candlemas

10

The Voices of the Wise

The Epiphany, 6 January, is one of the feasts that I have always loved, perhaps because I so often ended up as one of the kings in our school and church Nativity plays. The feast celebrates three wonders – the coming of the Magi, the baptism of Christ, and the first miracle at Cana – and recent liturgical material has made us much more aware of all three. Yet the most celebrated is still the coming of the Magi and at St Bartholomew the Great, as at a number of other churches, the Magi are gradually brought from the east end of the church to take their places beside the crib. In the medieval Church it seems to have been usual to wear vestments embroidered with stars – *vestimenta stellata* – for the Epiphany and one instruction from the fourteenth century says 'it does not matter of what colour the dalmatic and tunicle be, so long as they be sprinkled with stars'.

The only biblical material that directly concerns the Magi is that contained in Matthew 2.1–12. It tells that the *magoi* (this is the Greek word for sages) came from the East. The Latin Bible keeps the Greek word as it reports '*ecce Magi ab oriente*', 'Behold wise men from the East'. It was the theologian Tertullian, who died in 225, who called them kings and this designation became general in the sixth century on the basis of Psalm 72: 'The kings of Tharsis and of the isles shall give presents: the kings of Arabia and Saba shall bring gifts.' Because they gave three gifts, they are thought of as being three in number, though Matthew does not tell how many they were. From the sixth century the kings had names. These are most familiar in their Latin form of Caspar, Melchior and Balthasar. They were thought of as kings but also as sorcerers, astrologers, and philosophers, men of great wisdom. Already the tradition had begun to embroider the story, for the biblical account presented a great number of questions. Why did they go to Jerusalem? Why was Herod troubled? And why 'all Jerusalem' with him? Why did the star cease from guiding them and then reappear after they left Jerusalem? What sort of star was it? What was the meaning of the gifts they offered? What happened to them after they returned to their own country? The tradition has always been able to provide answers to these sorts of questions. It gives an answer after carefully considering every aspect of the issue, after weighing every possible solution. First it analysed words, though it often used a faulty etymology. Then it examined the meaning of the symbols, the signification of every recorded detail. It linked New Testament happenings to Old Testament happenings making particular use of the psalms, for it considered David to be a prophet. It used such scientific knowledge as it had. We must remember that it was Scripture that defined the way in which the world was seen, but Scripture was supplemented by Greek philosophy that had been transmitted to the Western world by way of Arab philosophers.

As we noted when looking at the appearance of the angel to Mary, medieval thinkers were fascinated by angels in much the same way that alien life-forms, 'real' and imaginary, fascinate some people today because they present the possibility of other and radically different worlds. The star fascinated them because it was not created in the beginning, as defined by Genesis 1, and it was not fixed in the firmament, in the crystal spheres encircling the earth that were proposed by Ptolemaic science. And this was not an idle reflection, for Jacobus da Voragine reported in the *Golden Legend* that the Magi saw a fivefold star – a material, a spiritual, an intellectual, a rational, and a supersubstantial star! A real star in the sky; the light of faith in their hearts; the angel that appeared to them, called, because of the brightness of its light, a star; the Blessed Virgin Mary, hailed in popular devotion as *Ave Maris Stella*, Hail! Star of the sea; and finally Christ himself, the bright and morning star.

The tradition testifies to an integration of the concrete and spiritual universes of a degree that we associate with Eastern religions rather than with Christianity. It also shows us a symbolic system that permeates all of life. The Christian tradition demonstrates as well that there are a diversity of ways of understanding the world and that science alone does not adequately interpret the world or make sense of what happens within it. The essential message of the Epiphany, reinforced by the miracle at Cana and the baptism of Jesus – both of which will be examined in the next chapter – is that it reveals God in man, male and female, and assures us that, after the incarnation, God is always to be found in our humanity, and that we cannot understand ourselves, the communities and societies to which we belong or the world in which we live apart from God. When we reach spiritual maturity death itself no longer threatens us.

A COLD COMING

One Epiphany a few years ago I went to visit a retired churchwarden in hospital. He was at this point seriously ill and we were deeply concerned about him. With some effort he thanked me for coming and responded warmly to the various greetings that I brought him. I gave him the last rites of the Church, anointed him, prayed with him, and bade him, in the words of Newman's translation of the Latin *Proficiscere anima Christiani*, 'Go forth upon thy journey, Christian soul'. He knew, and I could not fail to be aware, that he had set out on the last stage of his pilgrimage. The rites completed I looked around for something to read to him.

His Prayer Book was there and he had been reading the lections for Christmas and for the days following. I read him the Epiphany Gospel of the wise men and, afraid of a silence punctuated only by the harshness of his breathing and the electronic whirr of the saline drip, I turned to one of the books on his bedside table, to a volume of poetry. The table of contents looked inviting – the Lady of Shalott, Hiawatha's Wedding, Auden and Betjeman and Eliot. It was Eliot I chose, a poem for the Epiphany, 'Journey of the Magi'. It was years since I had read it or heard it read but as I began it flooded back and at the beginning I suddenly recalled the end, a page and a half away: I recalled it and regretted my choice, recalled it and knew there was no turning back.

There is no substitute for reading it and I commend it to you if you do not know it or have not read it for some time. It is in Eliot's collected poems. He tells, in the voice of one of them, of the cold coming of the Magi, and of how they found the place and the child. At the end of the poem, this Magus, this wise man, this king, recalls the events. He asks whether they had gone for a birth or a death. He had, he said, seen birth and death and thought they were different. Returned to his kingdom, and no longer at ease with the old gods, the Magus expresses a last thought: I would be glad of another death.

The words hung there in the hospital room, where his late wife's smiling face kept watch over him in his suffering; it was uttered and it was true. Eliot's Magus spoke and Peter, for that was his name, echoed it: 'I would be glad of another death.' But Peter was not afraid of death. Disturbed by the trouble, the inconvenience of a life coming to an end, disturbed but not afraid. To him the language of the Prayer Book and of its liturgy was entirely internalized; it was second nature. It was not something external, to be contemplated, but something inward and essential, something to be lived. And the resurrection of the body and the life everlasting were not abstract theological ideas, not insubstantial longings to bring comfort in grief, but certainties that defined both death and life. Worn out by illness and grief, Peter was glad of another death. I do not mean that he found it easy to let go, for life was for living and he had lived it, but dying too is an act of faith, an affirmation of our dependence, a resting on God, and the weekly affirmation of faith had prepared him for this last act. In this was true wisdom.

DIE DREI KÖNIGE

The story of the kings has probably attracted more artistic attention than any other aspect of the Christmas story except the Annunciation. A tradition developed of making one king old, one young, and the third black; In one Florentine painting deceased members of the Medici family take the roles – it was not commissioned by the Medici but by a sycophantic admirer. Whereas the shepherds find no one other than Mary, Joseph and the babe, with the possible addition of the midwives, often to be found drying cloths, there always seems to be a great crowd when the kings arrive, offering an opportunity to paint a diversity of rich robes. One of my favourite paintings of the Magi, in Washington, DC, has the farriers busy shoeing the visitors' horses. Their gifts of gold, frankincense and myrrh are also very familiar to us and the easily remembered words of 'We three kings' provided an effective interpretation of the meaning to be attributed to each of them. With the gift of myrrh we are again reminded of how the shadow of the cross falls over the Nativity. The *Golden Legend* offers additional interpretations, all of them possible. First, no one presented themselves empty-handed before a king, so the Magi, used to offering gifts, brought the finest produce of their land. Second comes St Bernard's practical suggestions – a very Cistercian solution – that the gold was given to relieve the poverty of the Blessed Virgin Mary, the frankincense to dispel the bad smells of the stable, and the myrrh as an ointment to strengthen the child's limbs and drive out worms! The third interpretation is that taken up in 'We three kings': the gold was offered as tribute to a king, the incense for worship and sacrifice, and the myrrh for burial of the dead, so that the gifts signify Christ's royal power, divine majesty, and human mortality. A fourth interpretation focuses on what we should offer Christ, love, symbolized by gold, prayer, symbolized by incense, and mortification of the flesh, symbolized by myrrh. And last, the gifts signify three attributes of Christ, namely, his most precious divinity, his most devout soul, and his intact and uncorrupted flesh.

There is a marvellous capital from the Cathedral of St Lazarus in Autun which is now housed in the cathedral museum. It shows the three kings in a bed with pillow and elaborate bedding wearing their crowns! Two are asleep, one is awake; his arm, outside the bedcover is being touched by a winged and haloed angel who is pointing into the distance and telling them to leave. There is something very gentle and dream-like about the angel. Matthew tells us that the kings returned by another route and the tradition includes the idea that they returned in three ships.

And what of the kings themselves? That proto-archaeologist, St Helena, the mother of the Emperor Constantine, is said to have brought their bodies from the East to Constantinople. Saint Eustorgius, Bishop of Milan – it is rather confusing that there were two bishops of this name, one in the fourth century and the other in the sixth – transferred the relics to Milan, and they were then removed to Cologne by the Emperor Frederick Barbarossa in 1162 or 1164. They were placed in the wonderful reliquary that still holds their bones and so became known as *die Drei Könige von Köln*, and their cult continues today with great veneration and devotion.

Relics may seem rather curious to us and to widely open to fraud, as followers of Brother Cadfael will be aware. But for our forebears, relics were of great importance because they held spiritual power. That power inhered in the saints' primary and secondary relics, that is, first of all in the physical remains, and secondly in personal possessions or in places. Though collecting relics may seem like our contemporary practice of gathering autographs or collecting memorabilia, the faithful believed – and not without evidence – that they provided access to the wonder-working saints in heaven.

Though not personally a great devotee of relics – however I have seen the well-attested relic of the True Cross at St Radegunde's monastery at Poitiers and the head of St John Baptist and a lot of others – I can say that it seems pretty unlikely that I would have been among the despoilers of shrines at the Reformation. I believe that we should take the physical and material aspects of our religion very seriously. To paraphrase C. S. Lewis: matter is important; God created it. I believe that we should pay careful attention to the way we handle the things that form the matter of the sacraments – the bread that is broken, the wine that is drunk, the oil liberally spread on those who are anointed, the water that fills the font, and the hands that are laid firmly on heads. I am also clear that paintings and statues and relics can mediate the divine presence.

Religion does not simply have spiritual effects. It also touches us in our bodily, physical existence. For example, if we look to the account of the exodus, we will find Moses listing the benefits of obedience – first on the journey: clothes that did not wear out, feet that did not swell – then at the journey's end: a land with flowing streams, wheat and barley, vines, fig trees and pomegranates, olive trees and honey. These are all material benefits. Moses does not say 'If you obey my commandments you will feel good, you will have a nice warm glow'. Quite the opposite – physical welfare, he says, depends on obedience to God. And even those commandments, set out in Deuteronomy, mostly concern material things – the dos and don'ts of eating, drinking, washing, cleaning, and so on.

The *Dreikönigenschrein* is dated between 1181 and 1230 and is a really magnificent example of the sort of great portable reliquary-shrine which could be carried in procession. It is studded with gem stones and cameos, many of them antique. There are little figures of the apostles and prophets on it, and at one end, where a removable golden plate enables the pilgrim to see the relics through a grill, Christ is depicted in majesty above, and below the kings offer their gifts to the Virgin at one side, while John baptizes Jesus on the other. Pilgrims must have felt themselves lifted up to heaven as they knelt in veneration before this shrine illuminated by countless flickering candles and received divine grace mediated through material things.

11

This is My Beloved Son

'Three wonders mark this holy day', declares the Epiphany liturgy, 'as the Church is joined to her heavenly Bridegroom', and each of the wonders reveals the divine nature of Jesus of Nazareth. 'This day a star leads the wise men to the manger. This day water is made wine at a wedding feast. This day Jesus is revealed as the Christ in the waters of baptism.' We have looked already at the visit of the Magi, and I want to think now about the other two wonders. The account of the marriage which 'Christ adorned and beautified by his presence and first miracle that he wrought, in Cana of Galilee' (familiar words from the marriage service) is contained only in John's Gospel. The baptism of Jesus by John the Baptist is recorded in the three Synoptic Gospels. I will begin at Cana.

THE FIRST MIRACLE THAT HE WROUGHT

As I observed in *Ashes to Glory*, there was a movement in the 1960s and 70s that approached the text of the Gospels with the idea that all accounts of miracles must be rejected. This view rested on a philosophical position which would not accept the possibility of miraculous intervention in a world ordered by laws discovered by science, for a miracle, by definition, violated these laws. Healing miracles could be explained in terms of psychology but turning water into wine, walking on water, and the feeding miracles could not be explained and so were, simply, straightforwardly, impossible. They were – it was argued – the product of a different culture, a culture that accepted miracles uncritically. Today we seem, if anything, to have an equally uncritical acceptance of the miraculous among certain groups within the Christian Church and a strong desire for such miracles outside the Church.

The liturgy establishes a pattern that shows us how the divine and the human, the spiritual and the material interact. The material world has its origin in God and is sustained by the divine will, but it has its own characteristics, its own freedom, its own laws. As I noted when considering the responsory *O magnum mysterium*, the liturgy stresses outward and visible material things as signs of inward and spiritual graces. In other words, the material world – as St Paul says – reveals the presence of God, but also, and more specifically shows God's love for and action towards us.

This action is sometimes marked by those events that we term miraculous, actions that go beyond our expectations, that move to the very edges of what is possible, to the limits of the natural world. Science can only deal with events that can be repeated, measured, and repeated again. God's one-off actions defy such measurement and repetition. They are not assured. They cannot be ordered. The divine will remains sovereign and cannot be manipulated. But we are given the means to be open to the power of God, means focused in and consolidated by the liturgy and the celebration of the sacraments. It is, I think, possible to affirm both the sovereignty of God and the freedom of the creation, but to see that God will, when he desires, use his power. The marriage feast at Cana shows us that divine power at work when exercised by the one who has the right to exercise it, by one who is here shown not only to exercise the sovereign power of God but to be God.

BY HIS PRESENCE IN CANA

Late in 1999 I officiated at a wedding in which the bridegroom was Anglican and the bride was Orthodox from Palestine. It provided another of those occasions in which one is led unexpectedly and delightfully to new understandings. Mervat, the bride, asked if certain features of the Orthodox service could be included in her wedding. She and her father, who had served as a cantor, took me through the various elements – the betrothal of the bride to the groom in the narthex (a space outside the church proper), the initial blessing by the priest, the untying of a ribbon placed across the entrance, the procession of bride and groom to the sanctuary, the presentation of the rings on a cushion, the crowning of the couple and the solemn blessings. My desire to do it well sent me to my books and in particular to the texts of the Orthodox marriage service. In the service itself I found new meaning in 'giving away' as Mervat's father entrusted her to Iain, the bridegroom, and in so doing surrendered that burden of care which parents traditionally maintain even for adult children.

Drawing on Orthodox texts assembled by Mark Searle and Kenneth Stevenson in *Documents on the Marriage Liturgy*, I prepared additional prayers for the wedding and particularly noticed the frequent references to the wedding at Cana. This was the proper preface from the Eucharist:

> *Through Jesus Christ our Lord,*
> *who is the blessed Spouse of thy Church,*
> *and as a guest at the wedding in Cana of Galilee,*
> *blessed the bridegroom and bride*
> *and made their goods abound;*
> *In thy mercy, therefore, O heavenly Father,*
> *may thy right hand,*
> *filled with all spiritual goodness,*
> *be placed upon the bridegroom and the bride*

> here before thee,
> that with angels and archangels,
> and with all the company of heaven,
> they may laud and magnify thy glorious Name,
> evermore praising thee, and saying: Holy, holy, holy ...

These words were spoken as the couples' crowns were removed:

> *Be exalted like Abraham, O Bridegroom,*
> *and be blessed like Isaac,*
> *and multiply like Jacob,*
> *walking in peace,*
> *and keeping God's commandments*
> *in righteousness.*
>
> *And you, O Bride,*
> *Be exalted like Sarah,*
> *and exult like Rebecca,*
> *and multiply like Rachel;*
> *and rejoice in your husband,*
> *according to those commandments*
> *that are well-pleasing to God.*
>
> *O God, our God,*
> *who didst come to Cana of Galilee,*
> *and didst bless there the marriage feast:*
> *Bless also these thy servants,*
> *who through thy good providence*
> *are now united in holy wedlock.*
> *Bless their going out and their coming in.*
> *Receive their crowns into thy kingdom,*
> *preserve them spotless, blameless,*
> *and without reproach,*
> *unto ages of ages. Amen.*

And these were the final blessings:

> *May the Father,*
> *and the Son,*
> *and the Holy Spirit,*
> *the all-holy,*
> *consubstantial,*
> *and life-giving Trinity,*
> *one Godhead and one Kingdom,*
> *bless you;*
> *and grant you length of days,*
> *fair children,*
> *progress in life and faith;*
> *and fill you with all earthly good things,*
> *and make you worthy to enjoy*
> *the good things of the promise;*
> *through the prayers of the holy Theotokos*
> [the God-bearer, one of Mary's titles]
> *and of all the saints. Amen.*

> *May he who by his presence in Cana of Galilee*
> *declared marriage to be honourable,*
> *Christ our true God,*
> *through the prayers of his most pure Mother;*
> *of the holy, glorious, and all laudable Apostles*
> *and of all the saints:*
> *have mercy on us and save us,*
> *for he is good and loves mankind. Amen.*

This moving experience made me think that, though I love the story of the wedding feast at Cana, and have often preached on it, I had not come anywhere near exhausting the richness of its meaning. Orthodox theology interprets it in a way that links us to the promise of God to Abraham and Sarah, to Isaac and Rebecca, to Jacob and Rachel, a promise of favour, land, descendants and greatness, and which makes Jesus Christ the concrete manifestation of that promise. And it is not just about the hereafter; it is about the here and now, where God is made manifest and where his disciples believe in him. So, then, what of the other manifestation?

I HAVE BAPTIZED YOU WITH WATER

The liturgy does not follow a chronological sequence. It does not re-enact the life of Christ in the way we might in a play. It is more like film or television, using flashbacks. As we have heard many voices calling to us in the last few weeks, so different strands have been developed in parallel or sometimes even doubling back to revisit earlier characters and events, to show that what happens later is the fulfilment of what was promised before. This is the case with John the Baptist. We heard his cry in the wilderness. We listened to the question that he put to Jesus through his disciples, now we see him as the baptizer. Mark's account of the baptism of Jesus is short and straightforward. It has very few details. It has, however, been a favourite of those who adorned fonts and baptisteries with sculpture and paintings, and the artists have provided the details. If you look at one or two of them, this is the sort of thing you will see:

There is John in his garment of camel-hair, marked by his long sojourn in the desert. There is the water piled up around Jesus, for the tradition includes the idea that the water moved, as it did when Israel crossed the Red Sea, when Joshua crossed the Jordan, and when Elisha struck the waters with the mantle of Elijah. There is Jesus, naked, standing in the water and modestly covered by it. John pours water over him, and the dove descends upon him. Above the dove, God the Father looks down from heaven, hand raised in benediction, and a banderolle gives the words: 'This is my beloved Son with whom I am well pleased.'

Thus far it is a pictorial representation of the biblical account, but we know well enough that our medieval forebears were much more fluent than we are in the language of sign and symbol. They understood symbols, interpreted events symbolically, and expressed their understanding by using and creating symbols. This gave them access to a number of levels of meaning, to a symbolic matrix which informs prayer, worship, poetry, art, architecture and sculpture, and even theology. So the artists and sculptors include ministering angels who sometimes look as if they are helpfully carrying towels, though perhaps they are just veiling their hands in a reverential gesture. They also put fish in the river. This is not just a realistic detail. The fish has long been associated with Christ since the Greek word for fish, ICTHUS, came to be understood as an acronym for Jesus Christ Son of God. But fish can also be seen as representing the souls that will be gathered into the nets of the fisherman turned disciples and fishers of men. One sculpture that I have seen shows a submerged human figure awaiting new birth by water and the spirit. In all these ways the baptismal sculptures stress the incarnation as 'for us and for our salvation'.

At Arezzo, in the tympanum of the church of Santa Maria, there are two trees in the depiction of the baptism. One is behind John, the other behind Jesus. John's tree is smaller and withered; Jesus' tree is rich with new growth. The trees are an obvious reference to the idea that John must decrease as Jesus increases. And John himself looking like Elijah, is seen as the last of the line of Jewish prophets, now supplanted by the appearance of the Son of God, as Hebrews says 'God, who at sundry times and in divers manners spake in time past unto the fathers by the prophets, hath in these last days spoken unto us by his Son.' (Hebrews 1.1 AV, used as the Epistle on Christmas Day in the Book of Common Prayer).

The most essential symbol points us back beyond the Law and the prophets to the very act of creation, to the Spirit of God brooding over the primeval waters. The baptism of Jesus is a new act of creation, a rebirth, as the Spirit is again manifest over the water and the Word addresses the Word. This is a moment of great drama. Of course the clouds must have been rent asunder. Of course there was a voice like thunder. Of course there were angels in attendance. 'Of course' because here God acts and acts definitively, and does so not merely 'for us and for our salvation' but to fulfil the promise made through Isaiah, to undo the curse of sin which affects even the ground and the trees and plants and animals. Our forebears placed humankind at the centre of the universe, from which place modern science and philosophy displaced us, but they also had a greater sense that the creation was more than us, a greater sense of unity and of integration. One reason for this was the closer link in their lives to natural cycles, to light and dark, to the seasons and the weather, to the vagaries of life before medical and scientific advances, to a profound awareness of changeability and mortality. The medievals knew that salvation had to mean salvation of and for the whole creation. We have only to look two verses on from the baptism to find Jesus in the wilderness with *but not devoured by* the wild beasts.

Among Renaissance artists the attitude to Jesus changes. It was part of that change from the wonderful patterns of Gothic art and sculpture, patterns that owed little to observation of the concrete world, to a greater awareness of what was really there. It is called 'renaissance' because it involved the recovery of classical insights, especially by observing classical sculpture and imitating it. The inner holiness and divine perfection must now be expressed in the human figure not by evoking timeless majesty through the use of gold or by making the divine and saintly figures larger than mere mortals but in the bodily appearance, in the real flesh. As one art historian observed, it was difficult for the medievals to remove the clothes of Christ when depicting his baptism for the clothes and their patterns expressed the nature of the person, but the Renaissance artist conceived the person as a nude and then clothed him or her. So Christ being baptized, as depicted, for example by Piero della Francesca in a painting in the National Gallery dating from the 1450s, has a tremendous bodily presence making us aware of his human perfection and revealing his divine nature.

Three voices are heard at the Jordan. The first is John. In Matthew's account he would have prevented Jesus being baptized saying, 'I need to be baptised by you, and do you come to me?' In this way John, the forerunner, pointed to the one who was greater than he. Also in Matthew's account Jesus says: 'Let it be so now; for thus it is fitting for us to fulfil all righteousness.' In this Jesus associates himself with sinful humanity, with those who, hearing John's call to repentance, have come to receive his baptism of forgiveness. Here we see his humility and willingness to accept whatever is necessary for salvation. The Gospel leads us to affirm what Paul teaches us in the letter to the Philippians (2.5–11):

Have this mind among yourselves, which is yours in Christ Jesus,
who, though he was in the form of God,
did not count equality with God a thing to be grasped,
but emptied himself, taking the form of a servant,
being born in the likeness of men.
And being found in human form he humbled himself
and became obedient unto death,
even death on a cross.
Therefore God has highly exalted him
and bestowed on him the name which is above every name,
that at the name of Jesus every knee should bow,
in heaven and on earth and under the earth,
and every tongue confess that Jesus Christ is Lord,
to the glory of God the Father.

And the third voice at the Jordan sets the scene for all that will follow: 'This is my Son, my beloved, with whom I am well pleased.'

12

A Light to Lighten the Gentiles

The National Gallery permanent collection includes a painting of
the event known as the Presentation of Christ in the Temple by
one of the leading painters of late fifteenth century Cologne. He is
known to us not by name but by title. He is called 'The Master of
the Life of the Virgin'. The panel in Trafalgar Square, oil paint on
oak, has become separated from the rest of the cycle, which is in
Munich. In this panel, 84 cm by $108\frac{1}{2}$ cm, the Temple lacks the
elaborate structure of apses, vaulting, and columns that we find in
the paintings of Giovanni di Paolo in Siena, Bartolo di Fredi in
the Louvre, or Ambrosio Lorenzetti in Florence. Here the Temple
is represented by a pavement of geometric design, a shimmering
golden wall, and an altar with a carved reredos. In the centre,
before the altar, a serene Mary, dressed in the deepest blue edged
in gold, hands a jolly baby to old Simeon. In that moment the
Christ-child is firmly held by four hands.

Behind Mary, to the left of the painting, stands Joseph
clutching a candle and, it seems, reaching in his pocket for an
offering. He too is depicted as an old man, and behind him is a
young woman clutching the pigeons, and three other 'supporters'
standing like friends and family at a baptism. The group of six
people on the right of the picture is not easily interpreted –
perhaps the woman wearing a turban is Anna the prophetess –
the remainder may be members of the family of the donor,
Johann von Hirtz.

The altar-cloth bears a Hebrew inscription. The altarpiece shows Abraham offering Isaac, Cain killing Abel, and the drunkenness of Noah. These are Old Testament scenes that were thought to prefigure Christ's sacrifice. Simeon's lovely cope has an embroidered hood which illustrates a quite different story. It is that of the Roman Emperor, Caesar Augustus. The senators, full of admiration for his rule and for the peace and prosperity of the whole world, come to him and say: 'We want to adore you, because there is divinity in you. If there were not, all fortunes would not lie subject to you.' Augustus was opposed to the idea of being worshipped and adored and asked for time to reflect upon it. He then called for the Tiburtine Sibyl to advise him. After three days she told him in the opaque verse favoured by oracles and soothsayers that a king would come from the heavens. This, it is said, took place in the Emperor's chamber on the Capitoline hill and there and then the heavens opened and a great light shone upon the Emperor. He saw in the sky a beautiful virgin, standing over an altar, holding a boy in her arms, and he heard a voice that said, 'This is the altar of the Son of God'. At that point Augustus fell to the ground in adoration.

The imperial chamber would become, in due course, the site of the church of Santa Maria in Capitolio, also known as Sancta Maria Ara Caeli, or, for brevity's sake, the Ara Caeli or altar of heaven. I must for a moment digress from the theme of Candlemas, for Christmas Day has always been observed with great solemnity at the Ara Caeli. The church possesses a delightful *Bambino*, a little wooden figure of the baby said to have been carved by a Franciscan friar in Jerusalem but finished by an angel! It is placed in a *presepio*, the traditional Italian manger which is to be seen in all Roman churches until after 2 February. Children would then come on 26 December to recite various pieces of poetry and prose in honour of the infant Jesus. On the Feast of the Epiphany a blessing is given with the *Bambino* from the steps of the church – a very long and impressive flight built in gratitude that Rome escaped the Black Death – which an immense crowd comes to witness. In this way the tradition of Augustus's vision is continued in a church built by Pope Gregory the Great in 591, possibly on the site of a church erected by the Emperor Constantine.

The painting in the National Gallery depicts the biblical scene but also links it to the Jewish and Roman worlds. This is not merely an event that draws its significance from Old Testament typology and biblical prophecy, it also fulfils the hopes of the pagan world and fulfils the prophecy of the Sibyls. And the painting does not just reflect the past. It relates it to the present and especially to the worship offered by the Church. The child is handled with the care and reverence with which the Sacred Host is offered at the Christian altar during the Mass. He alone is obviously haloed. Mary's halo is almost invisible but Christ's halo is like a sun-burst. The biblical scenes give an interpretation of the presentation of Christ that is consistent with Jewish expectation. Simeon's cope shows that it goes beyond the Jews to embrace the Gentiles and that the Christ-child is indeed a light to lighten the nations. Candlemas concludes the great Advent-Christmas-Epiphany cycle in the liturgy and moves us steadily towards Easter. The Christ-child is still in his mother's arms but she is already making an offering of him.

AS IT IS WRITTEN IN THE LAW OF THE LORD

The feast falling on 2 February is called the Presentation of Christ, or the Purification of the Blessed Virgin Mary, and is commonly known, because of the ceremonies related to it, as Candlemas. It is 40 days since the birth of Jesus. He has been circumcised according to the Law on the eighth day, that is on 1 January. Now Mary comes to the Temple to fulfil the requirement set down in Leviticus 12.2–8.

If a woman conceives and bears a male child, she shall be ceremonially unclean seven days; as at the time of her menstruation, she shall be unclean. On the eighth day the flesh of his foreskin shall be circumcised. Her time of blood purification shall be thirty-three days; she shall not touch any holy thing, or come into the sanctuary, until the days of her purification are completed. If she bears a female child, she shall be unclean two weeks, as in her menstruation; her time of blood purification shall be sixty-six days.

When the days of her purification are completed, whether for a son or for a daughter, she shall bring to the priest at the entrance of the tent of meeting a lamb in its first year for a burnt offering, and a pigeon or a turtledove for a sin offering. He shall offer it before the LORD, *and make atonement on her behalf; then she shall be clean from her flow of blood. This is the law for her who bears a child, male or female. If she cannot afford a sheep, she shall take two turtledoves or two pigeons, one for a burnt offering and the other for a sin offering; and the priest shall make atonement on her behalf, and she shall be clean.*

Mary had no need to submit to the Law but she did, and it was St Bernard who noted the symmetry here: Jesus had no need of circumcision as a sign of the covenant and Mary no need of purification but both accepted obedience to the Law in humility. The *Golden Legend*, following Bernard, says that Jesus was a poor man by birth and in his circumcision he accepted the common human burden of sin. At the presentation, the offering of the poor is made – two young pigeons, Mary accepts purification, and Jesus the act of being redeemed. Later, though without sin, he will accept, as we have already seen, John's baptism of repentance. In all things, therefore, Christ chose to accept the remedies established against original sin not because he had need of them but in humility and in solidarity with sinful humankind.

THE MEETING

One of the less well-known titles of this feast is *hypopanti*, the meeting, because of the meetings between the Christ-child and his parents and Simeon and Anna. From the meeting with Simeon comes that most beloved of canticles, the Nunc dimittis. Simeon and Anna first of all show God at work under the old covenant. It is too easy for us to read the New Testament account of the synagogue and the criticisms of the scribes and lawyers and of the Pharisees as if there was no religious vitality and no true devotion. This is clearly not the case and there are a number of examples of true devotion, not least Elizabeth and Zechariah, Mary and Joseph, and Simeon and Anna. Simeon is specifically described as 'righteous and devout' and we are told that the Holy Spirit was upon him. This also shows us the Spirit at work before the great outpouring of Pentecost and reminds us of how far the Spirit went in preparing for the coming of Christ. It was the Spirit that led Simeon to the Temple on that day. We do not know how many came to the Temple to present their children or how Simeon knew which one was the Lord's Christ but, as we have already seen in the painting, he took the child in his arms and blessed God and said, 'Lord, now lettest thou thy servant depart in peace'.

What Simeon is saying to God is that he may now be allowed to die because he knows that he has seen what the Lord promised, the Messiah, the Christ, the beginning of the working out of the plan of salvation. Simeon calls the child 'salvation', 'light' and 'glory'. Salvation here belongs to the whole world; the light comes as revelation to the Gentiles, to those who sit in darkness; the glory belongs to Israel as God fulfils his promise made through the prophets. Simeon then turns to Mary and Joseph who were marvelling at what he said and tells Mary that this child is 'set for the fall and rising of many in Israel' and that a sword will pierce through her own soul. I have already observed at

several points the way in which the shadow of the cross falls over
the Christ-child. I cannot hear the words of Simeon's prophecy
without thinking of the hymn *Stabat Mater dolorosa* attributed to
the thirteenth century Franciscan mystic and writer Jacopone da
Todi (though also to Pope Innocent III and to St Bonaventure).
The best-known English version renders the first stanza in this
way:

> *At the Cross her station keeping*
> *Stood the mournful Mother weeping,*
> *Where he hung, the dying Lord;*
> *For her soul, of joy bereavèd,*
> *Bowed with anguish, deeply grievèd,*
> *Felt the sharp and piercing sword.*

Anna is often ignored in the account of the presentation. She is an
observer of the scene but she too, prepared by long periods of
prayer and fasting, knew what it was she saw. She shows us, as
Luke intended, that it is not enough to see Christ and to know
that he is Christ. The good news has to be shared and she spoke of
him to 'all who were looking for the redemption of Jerusalem'.

THE SOUL CONCEALED IN FAT FLESH

The feast is also called Candlemas. The Mass traditionally began
with the blessing of candles and a procession. Rather like the old
blessing of palms and branches of olive on Palm Sunday, which
invoked all the symbolic aspects of the trees, the medieval blessing
of candles involved multiple prayers. As the candles were taken
home and were believed to carry with them the blessing imparted
during the ceremony the first prayer asks that the candles may
bring health of body and soul to those who carry them. It also
recalls the wonder of the medievals at the way in which by the
labour of bees the liquid comes to the perfection of wax. The

same theme is taken up in the blessing of the Paschal Candle at Easter. The second concludes with a petition that those who bear the candles might be 'inflamed by the fire of thy most sweet charity'. The third points to the invisible fire illuminating our hearts, as the visible fire dispels the darkness. The fourth, though a blessing over candles, refers to oil lamps prepared by Moses to burn continuously before the Lord, and so perhaps points to an older practice of lighting lamps rather than candles. And the fifth summarizes all the petitions that the light and fire of the Holy Spirit may enlighten us and enable us to acknowledge and to love God. During the singing of the Nunc dimittis the candles were distributed and during the procession antiphons were sung which, taken from the Greek liturgy, show the extent to which the Roman liturgy maintained some older traditions, and brought them in its missionary expansion from the East to all parts of Christendom. It may surprise us to know that the Christians of medieval England regularly sang chants from the Greek Church. The liturgical texts do not, of course, tell us anything of the procession except that it happened and we must imagine clergy and ministers in their vestments, incense rising from the thurible, and ordinary Christians clutching their candles passing through the aisles and arches of ancient churches, their faces illuminated by the gentle flickering light.

Perhaps, as the *Golden Legend* frankly admits, this procession of blessed candles was a deliberate Christian response to the way that the Romans honoured Februa, the mother of Mars, by lighting the city with candles and torches throughout the night, or the feast of lights that recalled the search for the abducted Proserpina (Spring) as the days began to lengthen again. The Roman celebration survived but with an altered meaning. Another reason for the procession was to recall the procession of Mary, Joseph, Simeon and Anna, as they presented Jesus. The lighted candle which each person carries signifies Jesus being borne into the church. The candle, with its wick, wax and fire, represents three things about

Christ: 'the wax is a sign of his body, which was born of the Virgin Mary without corruption of the flesh, as bees make honey without mingling with each other; the wick signifies his most pure soul, hidden in his body; the fire stands for his divinity, because God is a consuming fire.' This was all expressed in a Latin verse translated in this way:

> *This candle I carry in honour of holy Mary.*
> *Take the wax for the true body born of the Virgin.*
> *Take the light for God and his supreme majesty.*
> *Take the wick for the soul concealed in the fat flesh.*

AND LET ALL SPORTS WITH CHRISTMAS DIE

As I noted a little earlier, the Christmas cribs are still in place in the churches of Rome on 2 February. I have never subscribed to the view that decorations should be taken down on Twelfth Night and the idea that they should be was probably part of an attempt to get people back to work after the prolonged mid-winter season of holy days. In the Middle Ages the Christmas doxology was ordered to be sung at the end of all hymns until the morrow of Candlemas. At Lichfield the church was hung with silk curtains from Christmas to Candlemas according to the statute of 1194, and this custom of letting the Christmas decorations remain up until that feast (or until Septuagesima, should that fall first) seems to have been fairly general all over England until at least the mid-seventeenth century or even later, for Dean Swift, writing on Candlemas 1711–12, says, 'This ends Christmas and what care I?' Overall the liturgical evidence suggests that there were two periods which can be termed Christmastide: the one lasting till the octave of the Epiphany, that is to 13 January, after which the colour of vestments and hangings was changed and the weekday services lost their festal character; the other lasting on till Candlemas (or Septuagesima, the third Sunday before Lent begins, if that fell first), during which the Christmas doxology was continued and the decorations remained up.

I am always sad to see Christmas end, for it is a season that I love. The poet and clergyman Robert Herrick, who longed, in the days of Cromwell's Commonwealth, for the joys of Old England, shared that sentiment. His Candlemas verses combine the traditions of the Yule log and the evergreen decorations with his sense that the presence of Christ throughout the year protects from evil and I will, therefore, allow him to end these reflections for me:

Ceremony upon Candlemas Eve

> *Down with rosemary, and so*
> *Down with the bays and mistletoe;*
> *Down with the holly, ivy, all*
> *Wherewith ye dressed the Christmas Hall:*
> *That so the superstitious find*
> *No one least branch there left behind:*
> *For look, how many leaves there be*
> *Neglected, there (maids, trust to me)*
> *So many Goblins you shall see.*

The Ceremonies for Candlemas Day

> *Kindle the Christmas brand, and then*
> *Till Sunset let it burn;*
> *Which quench'd, then lay it up again*
> *Till Christmas next return.*
> *Part must be kept wherewith to teend*
> *The Christmas log next year,*

> *And where 'tis safely kept, the fiend*
> *Can do no mischief there*

Upon Candlemas Day

> *End now the white-loaf and the pie,*
> *And let all sports with Christmas die.*

Appendix

The Structure of Advent and Christmas

One Advent Sunday morning, when I was a theological student, I greeted the curate of St Peter and St Paul, Battersea, in south London, with the words 'Happy New Year!' After his initial surprise, he recognized that I was talking about the beginning of the Church's new liturgical year. The Book of Common Prayer began the 'Collects, Epistles and Gospels to be used throughout the year' with that of the First Sunday in Advent and the first Mass of the Roman Missal was for that same Sunday. The books that set out the customs of medieval monasteries usually began '*Sabbato adventus domini ad vesperas*' and gave the instructions for Vespers on the Saturday evening prior to Advent Sunday. There were other places of starting – Christmas Day, the civil new year on 1 January, or on 25 March. This latter was really the most significant of all days for it was calculated to be that of Christ's conception, of his death and of the creation of the world!

Advent gradually claimed to be the beginning of the new cycle and it seems so well settled that it may be a surprise to discover that liturgical scholars are perplexed by it. The historical evidence concerning its origin and original purpose is conflicting and inconclusive. Before the liturgical reforms of the period 1960–80 the liturgy of the Roman Catholic Church was a modified version of the medieval liturgy. The ancient Roman liturgy had been brought to England by St Augustine at the end of the sixth century and we can see its influence on the Book of Common

Prayer when we note how many saints of the city of Rome are included in the calendar. Before the Second Vatican Council in the 1960s, the Roman liturgy had developed over the centuries with the gradual addition of new feasts and celebrations. One influential commentator, Pius Parsch, contrasted the older and newer feasts. The former, he said, were like virgin forests; the latter, like artistically kept flower gardens. Something rather similar can be said of the Advent liturgy and the way it has developed.

Another way of looking at it could be drawn from the study of architecture. I happen to be very interested in Norman or Romanesque architecture, partly because St Bartholomew the Great retains a lot of original Norman features. The architectural historian Hans Erich Kubach says of Romanesque that 'it proves to be a new creation which utilised and transformed whatever stimuli were received from elsewhere' and when we compare it with what went before – in Egypt, Palestine, Syria, Asia Minor, Armenia and Byzantium, or with parallel developments in Armenia and Russia – 'we find that there is often a disconcerting similarity but very rarely anything we can define as a truly tangible relationship'. The Advent and Christmas liturgies of the Western Church are built on a site which had already both pagan and Christian buildings standing on it. There are Eastern influences, from the Greek Church. There are creative interchanges between papal Rome and the Franco-Germanic world of the Emperor Charlemagne. There are some influences, like that of the processions and stational churches of the city of Rome, which are slight and yet which contribute something distinctive to the whole. The Advent liturgy is a new creation which nevertheless used and reused whatever was available for the project and transformed it in the process. The existing buildings – notably the feast of the Epiphany, the Ember Days, and some of the older saints' days, were incorporated into the new structure, modified, extended and enabled to serve a new function.

THE ORIGIN AND STRUCTURE OF ADVENT

The traditional liturgical year pivots on two points, Christmas and Easter. The former has a fixed date and therefore a variable day: it is always 25 December but it can fall on any day of the week, including Sunday. The latter is always on a Sunday and has a variable date ranging from 22 March to 25 April. Some early liturgical books begin with the Masses of Christmas day rather than those of Advent. As the liturgy develops, the length of the pre-Christmas period varies. It can be as short as one Sunday or as long as six or seven. In Spain, it was, like Lent, of 40 days duration and so began on 16 November. In Gaul (modern France), the opening day was the feast of St Martin, 11 November, and it was known as *Quadragesima sancti Martini*, St Martin's Lent. Within the Empire of Charlemagne and his successors there are traces of a three-month period of preparation beginning on the feast of the Conception of St John the Baptist, 24 September. In Rome, it seems to have been first six weeks in duration, then five, and finally settled to four. This four-Sunday scheme was normal throughout most of the Latin Church by the tenth century and it passed by way of the Sarum Use (the liturgical practice of the Cathedral Church of Salisbury which was used widely throughout England) into the Book of Common Prayer.

Advent therefore has a variable length in terms of number of days, ranging from twenty-one to twenty-eight. It is possible for the Fourth Sunday to be Christmas Eve, as shown in this table:

	Advent 1	Advent 2	Advent 3	Advent 4
Earliest	27 November	4 December	11 December	18 December
Latest	3 December	10 December	17 December	24 December

In non-religious observance in the West today the period of preparation for Christmas has been pushed back to the end of October (though I saw a notice asking 'Have you stocked up for Christmas' in September 1999) but Advent has become coterminous with the 24 days of December prior to Christmas to enable secular 'Advent calendars' to begin on 1 December every year.

The following two columns may begin to indicate some of the difficulties involved in aligning the Sundays of Advent with the dates on which the season can begin. The right-hand column has to slide to align its beginning with the date on which the first Sunday falls. The sequence will then be truncated by the position in the week of Christmas Day. After Christmas Day itself the Sundays and dated feasts still have to be correlated. The Sunday can fall on any of the days in the week after Christmas and there can be one or two Sundays before we reach the Epiphany. At the far end of the cycle, Candlemas can be in the pre-Lent period.

Fixed dates	Moveable days
November	FIRST SUNDAY IN ADVENT
27	M
28	T
29 Vigil of St Andrew	W
30 St Andrew, Apostle	Th
December	Fr
1	Sa
2	SECOND SUNDAY IN ADVENT
3	M
4	T
5	W
6 St Nicholas	Th
7	Fr

8	The Immaculate Conception of the Blessed Virgin Mary	Sa	

THIRD SUNDAY IN ADVENT

9		M	
10		T	
11		W	Ember Day
12		Th	Ember Day
13	St Lucy	Fr	
14		Sa	Ember Day

15		**FOURTH SUNDAY IN ADVENT**
16	*O Sapientia*	*This may also be Christmas Eve*
17		M	*Christmas may fall*
18		T	*on any day this week*
19		W	
20	Vigil of St Thomas	Th	
21	St Thomas, Apostle	Fr	
22		Sa	
23		Su	*This will be the First Sunday after Christmas, if it is not Christmas Day*
24	Vigil of Nativity		
25	Christmas Day	M	
26	St Stephen	T	
27	St John	W	
28	The Holy Innocents	Th	
29	St Thomas of Canterbury	Fr	
30		Sa	
31	St Silvester	Su	*This can be (a) the First Sunday after Christmas, (b) the Second Sunday after Christmas, or (c) the First Sunday after the Epiphany*

January
1 The Circumcision of our Lord

THE CHARACTER OF THE SEASONS

In the Gallican (French) church, Advent always had, it seems, an ascetic and penitential nature. In the Roman Church, that is the Church of the City of Rome, it had a purely liturgical character. In the liturgical interchange that created the medieval liturgy, the Romano-Frankish Advent became a season of four Sundays with a penitential character, though never as deeply penitential as Lent. Fasting was limited to the Ember days and there were few other ascetical practices. In general, the joyful chants, the *Gloria in excelsis* ('Glory be to God on high'/'Glory to God in the highest') and the *Te Deum* ('We praise thee, God'/'You are God and we praise you') were omitted. The Alleluia between the Epistle and Gospel was still sung. Purple vestments were worn in Rome, with rose-coloured vestments, including dalmatic and tunicle, on the third Sunday (when the introit began *Gaudete*, 'Rejoice in the Lord always'). In England it was rather different: white was worn in Advent at Westminster Abbey, blue at Wells, and violet at Exeter, perhaps under the Roman influence of Bishop Grandisson who was Chaplain to Pope John XXII at Avignon. The Sarum *Ordinale* – the book that sets out the customs of the different seasons and the liturgical texts to be used in the churches that followed the use of Salisbury – orders the wearing of chasubles, rather than dalmatics and tunicles, by the deacon and subdeacon at High Mass, but says nothing of the colour. It here means folded chasubles. The chasuble was the common vestment of all ministers and it was folded to facilitate the deacon's functions, freeing his hands and arms, but when the dalmatic became the normal diaconal vestment the folded chasuble was associated with penitential seasons.

The preface to the 1991 publication of the Church of England Liturgical Commission *The Promise of His Glory* provided an excellent summary of the Church's position through Advent and Christmas. It acknowledged that the season of Christmas is the focal point of religious observance for many people. It recognizes that the period from Advent to Candlemas does not contain a chronological sequence of events in Christ's life and that there is no ancient sequence of rites to be followed or even a consensus among Christians past and present about keeping the various feasts. And our present observance is affected by the 'tinsel-clad shopping days' that begin in mid-December and by the anticipated celebration of Christmas at carol services and concerts, in schools and civic centres, well in advance of the blessing of the crib and the Midnight Mass.

Christmas breaks upon us sooner or later as a season of celebration and gold and white, and indeed the best of any colour, replace the penitential garb. The *Gloria in excelsis* is restored and the festival continues, as we will see, until Epiphany, the octave day of the Epiphany (13 January) or until Candlemas on 2 February.

EXPLORING ADVENT

Liturgical reform and renewal has had its effect on the season of Advent. The building site has been effectively cleared of earlier structures and general principles belonging to the whole year have been applied to this season as well. In 1969 the Roman Catholic Church affirmed the twofold character of Advent as the preparation for Christmas and the turning of our minds to Christ's second coming. Advent stayed the same length and the special orientation of the weekdays, 17 to 24 December, was retained. The season was described as a period of devout and joyful expectation and as such the Roman Church looked for moderation in music and in floral decoration. The Advent Ember Days were removed and so was the feast of St Thomas the Apostle. With the exception of the Immaculate Conception there was to be no feast above the rank of a memorial during December. Advent has become a less interesting place to explore and that is why I have deliberately gone back behind the reforms.

This investigation of the liturgical voices of Advent and Christmas, of the Epiphany and of Candlemas, draws heavily on my study of medieval liturgy. The texts that I have used are drawn from the Mass and Offices of the Latin Church, together with prayers, hymns, sermons, the lives of the saints, and writings about the seasons. I have sat with a diverse collection of missals, breviaries and processionals, hymnals and carol books, art books and museum guides open in front of me as I have been writing and I have listened again to recordings of traditional Advent and Christmas music. It allows one to enter a sort of shadow world. As the churches have abandoned much that can be counted as traditional, so it has been picked up by others, including those who, finding little to delight them liturgically in modern churches, reconstruct ancient liturgies.

It may help if I explain something of my approach and about the terms that I use. The medieval Church used Latin and the liturgy is rich in texts written in that language. There has in consequence been a lot of Latin, and a little Greek, in these chapters. Hebrew, Greek and Latin were used for the superscription on the cross and their linguistic and semantic characters shape doctrine and liturgy. English translations rarely catch the terse poetic nature of the Latin original. Quite a lot of the English has been drawn from the Book of Common Prayer 1662, from the Coverdale Psalter used with it, from the Authorized Version, and from traditional hymns found in the older hymnbooks and some more modern ones.

I find that I have often used the expression 'the tradition'. When I do so I am distinguishing a strand in the Church's life that shapes and informs our worship from that which is found in Scripture and in the Catholic Creeds. The Scriptures, the books of the Old and New Testaments, together with the Apocrypha, are called the Canon, literally 'the rule', containing all that is necessary for salvation. 'The tradition' is a body of teaching and writing – an extremely extensive collection in many languages and from many periods – that comments on, and seeks to elucidate Scripture and the Creeds, together with pious opinions, histories, legends, and stories that expand on Scripture, fill in the gaps and provide imaginative (and often imaginary) extra details. A good example of the tradition is the *Golden Legend* of Jacobus da Voragine. It is a collection of teachings and stories linked to the liturgical year and especially to the saints. Jacobus includes any story that he has heard or read and liked, and we often find him reporting what has been said or taught and then saying that it can't be true or he doesn't believe it or there is another version that contradicts it and he can't choose between them.

THE LITURGICAL MATERIAL

The liturgy of the medieval Church can be divided into the Mass (Eucharist) and the Divine Office. Our Morning and Evening Prayer (Mattins and Evensong) derive from the offices sung during the day. The only texts that really interest me in the Mass, for my present purposes, are the introits, sung at the beginning of the celebration, and the Alleluia, sung before the Gospel. The collection of texts making up the proper of the Mass for a given occasion was often known by the opening words of the introit. The third Sunday of Advent is called Gaudete Sunday because the introit begins *Gaudete in Domino semper*, 'Rejoice in the Lord alway'.

The Office is much richer in texts because it uses a number of different antiphons, responsories and hymns. These are particularly to be found in Nocturns, the night office which is sometimes, confusingly, called Mattins. The equivalent of our Mattins is Lauds and of our Evensong, Vespers. Sunday began on Saturday with First Vespers. Antiphons are sentences, usually taken from Scripture, that are sung before and after the Psalms and Canticles

(Benedictus at Lauds and Magnificat at Vespers) in the Divine Office. By way of example, here are the antiphons from Vespers and Lauds of the First Sunday in Advent in parallel Latin and English texts:

In illa die stillabunt montes dulcedinum, et colles fluent lac et mel, alleluia.

In that day the mountains shall drop down sweetness, and the hills shall flow with milk and honey, alleluia.

Jucundare, filia Sion, et exsulta satis, filia Jerusalem, alleluia.

Rejoice, O daughter of Sion, and shout for joy, O daughter of Jerusalem, alleluia.

Ecce Dominus veniet, et omnes Sancti ejus cum eo et erit in die illa lux magna, alleluia.

Behold the Lord shall come, and all his Saints with him and there shall be on that day a great light, alleluia.

Omnes sitientes, venite ad aquas: quaerite Dominum, dum inveniri potest, alleluia.

All you that thirst, come to the waters: seek ye the Lord while he may be found, alleluia.

Ecce veniet Propheta magnus, et ipse renovabit Jerusalem, alleluia.

Behold there shall come a great Prophet, and he shall restore Jerusalem, alleluia.

The antiphon sung before the Benedictus or the Magnificat is usually longer and not always biblical. This is the splendid Magnificat antiphon for Christmas Day:

Hodie Christus natus est: hodie Salvator apparuit: hodie in terra canunt Angeli, laetantur Archangeli: hodie exsultant iusti, dicentes: Gloria in excelsis Deo, alleluia.

Today Christ is born, today the Saviour has appeared; today Angels are singing on earth; Archangels are rejoicing; today the just are glad and say: Glory to God in the highest, alleluia.

It has inspired a number of composers and my favourite settings of this and other antiphons are by Francis Poulenc.

There is a short response at the end of office hymns and certain psalms; it has a verse and a response. This one is used for hymns throughout Advent at Lauds:

V. *Vox clamantis in deserto: Parate viam Domini.*

V. *A voice crying in the wilderness: Prepare the way of the Lord.*

R. *Rectas facite semitas.*

R. *Make straight his paths.*

And this one at Vespers:

V. *Rorate, caeli, desuper, et nubes pluant justum.*

V. *Drop down dew, ye heavens, from above, and let the clouds rain the just.*

R. *Aperiatur terra, et germinet Salvatorem.*

R. *Let the earth be opened and bud forth a Saviour.*

The short reading, called a Chapter, also has a responsory. This is set for the Sunday after Christmas Day:

V. *Verbum caro factum est, Alleluia, aleluia.*

V. *The Word was made flesh, Alleluia, alleluia.*

R. *Verbum caro factum est, Alleluia, alleluia.*

R. *The Word was made flesh, Alleluia, alleluia.*

V. *Et habitavit in nobis.*

V. *And dwelt among us.*

R. *Alleluia.*

R. *Alleluia.*

V. *Gloria patri.*

V. *Glory be to the Father, etc.*

R. *Verbum caro factum est, Alleluia, alleluia.*

R. *The Word was made flesh, Alleluia, alleluia.*

The longest form of responsory is used during Nocturns. This is an example from the Christmas Offices, found in the first Nocturn of Christmas and partially repeated at Lauds on Christmas morning:

V. *Quem vidistis, pastores? dicite, annuntiate nobis, in terris quis apparuit?*

V. *Whom have you seen, O shepherds? Speak and tell us, who has appeared on earth?*

R. *Natum vidimus, et choros Angelorum collaudantes Dominum.*

R. *'We saw the new-born Child and choirs of angels, loudly praising the Lord.'*

V. *Dicite, quidnam vidistis? et annuntiate Christi nativitatem.*

V. *Speak what have you seen? And tell us of the birth of Christ.*

R. *Natum vidimus, et choros Angelorum collaudantes Dominum.*

R. *'We saw the new-born Child and choirs of angels, loudly praising the Lord.'*

The *Quem vidistis* with its dialogue form provided a beginning for medieval drama. People soon found that they wanted to act out the dialogues and move around the church as they did so, and a number of liturgical plays began in that way.

These texts sung in the Mass and Offices shape the liturgical seasons. They also create a series of connections and resonances, linking the prophets to the Psalms and to the Gospels and providing a commentary on them. Some of them are known to us because they have reappeared as hymns, or are found in pieces of music, or else have returned to us through the current process of liturgical enrichment.

Notes on Sources and Further Reading

I began to explore the Advent and Christmas voices in an essay *'Vox clara*: The Liturgical Voice in Advent and Christmas' in Martin Dudley, editor, *Like a two-edged sword: The Word of God in Liturgy and History*, Canterbury Press, Norwich 1995.

The early liturgical history is set out in J. Neil Alexander, *Waiting for the Coming: the liturgical meaning of Advent, Christmas and Epiphany*, The Pastoral Press, Washington, D.C., 1993, and, in greater scholarly detail by Prof. Alexander's mentor Thomas J. Talley in *The Origins of the Liturgical Year*, The Liturgical Press, Collegeville 1991.

The commentary on the pre-Vatican II Roman Liturgy by Pius Parsch is in the first volume of his work *The Church's Year of Grace*, The Liturgical Press, Collegeville 1957, and that by Aemiliana Löhr in *The Mass Through The Year* (vol. 1) London, 1958.

Though there are many modern books on the history of Christmas and its customs the best is still Clement A. Miles, *Christmas in Ritual and Tradition Christian and Pagan*, London 1912. There is also much fascinating material (including The Second Shepherds' Play) in *The Roads from Bethlehem: A Christmas Anthology*, SPCK 1994.

Quotations from the Fathers of the Church are largely taken from volume 1 (Advent and Christmastide) of *A Word in Season*, Talbot

Press, Dublin 1973, edited by Henry Ashworth OSB. *The Golden Legend* is available in a readable two-volume translation by William Granger Ryan, Princeton University Press 1993. *The Lauds* of Jacopone da Todi, translated by Serge and Elizabeth Hughes, is published in the Classics of Western Spirituality series, SPCK 1982.

The Orthodox wedding texts were derived from those in Mark Searle and Kenneth Stevenson, *Documents of the Marriage Liturgy*, The Liturgical Press, Collegeville 1992.

There are several essays about the Boy Bishop and the Feast of the Holy Innocents, including my own '*Natalis innocentum*: the Holy Innocents in liturgy and drama', in Diana Wood, editor, *The Church and Childhood*, Ecclesiastical History Society/Blackwell 1994.

Robert Herrick's verses and much other marvellous material for Christmas reflection can be found in D. B. Wyndham-Lewis and G. C. Heseltine, *A Christmas Book*, London 1928 and numerous subsequent editions.

There are excellent photographs of many of the paintings to which I have referred in the National Gallery volume by Jill Dunkerton, Susan Foster, Dillian Gordon and Nicholas Penny, *Giotto to Dürer: Early Renaissance Painting in the National Gallery*, National Gallery Publications 1991.

Bibliography

Alexander, J. Neil, *Waiting for the Coming: The Liturgical Meaning of Advent, Christmas and Epiphany*. The Pastoral Press, Washington, D.C., 1993.

American Book of Common Prayer. Church Hymnal Corporation, New York, 1979.

Ashworth, Henry, OSB (ed.), *A Word in Season*. Talbot Press, Dublin, 1973.

Coulton, G. G., *Life in the Middle Ages*. Vol. 1. Cambridge, Cambridge University Press, 1967.

da Todi, Jacopone, *The Lauds*. trans. Serge and Elizabeth Hughes, Classics of Western Spirituality, SPCK, London, 1982 and Paulist Press, Ramsey, N.J., 1982.

Dudley, Martin, *Ashes to Glory: Meditations for Lent, Holy Week and Easter*. SPCK, London, 1999.

Dudley, Martin (ed.), *Like a Two-Edged Sword: The Word of God in Liturgy and History*. Canterbury Press, Norwich, 1995.

Dudley, Martin, '*Natalis innocentum*: the Holy Innocents in liturgy and drama', in Diana Wood (ed.), *The Church and Childhood*. Ecclesiastical History Society/Blackwell, Oxford, 1994.

Dunkerton, J., Foster, S., Gordon, D. and Penny, N., *Giotto to Dürer: Early Renaissance Painting in the National Gallery*. National Gallery Publications, London, 1991.

Eliot, T. S., *Four Quartets, Collected Poems 1909–1962*. Faber & Faber, London, 1963.

Farrer, A., *Said or Sung: An Arrangement of Homily and Verse*. Faith Press, London, 1960.

Golden Legend, The. trans. William Granger Ryan, Princeton University Press, Princeton, N. J., 1993.

Guerric of Igny, *Liturgical Sermons I*. Cistercian Fathers Series, Kalamazoo, 1971.

Herrick, Robert, *The Poetical Works of Robert Herrick*. Ed. F. W. Moorman. Oxford University Press, Oxford, 1921.

Löhr, Aemiliana, *The Mass Through the Year*, Vol. 1. Longmans, Green, London, 1958.

Miles, Clement A., *Christmas in Ritual and Tradition Christian and Pagan*. T. Fisher Unwin, London, 1912.

Monastic Diurnal, The. H. Dessain, Mechlin, 1963.

Parsch, Pius, *The Church's Year of Grace*. The Liturgical Press, Collegeville, 1957.

Poston, Elizabeth (ed.), *The Penguin Book of Christmas Carols*. Penguin Books, Harmondsworth, 1965.

Ratzinger, J., *Dogma and Preaching*. Franciscan Herald Press, Chicago, 1985.

Searle, Mark and Stevenson, Kenneth (eds.), *Documents of the Marriage Liturgy*. The Liturgical Press, Collegeville, 1992.

Stern, J. P., *Hitler: The Führer and the People*. Fontana, London, 1984.

Talley, Thomas J., *The Origins of the Liturgical Year*. The Liturgical Press, Collegeville, 1991.

Troiano, Edna M., *The Roads from Bethlehem: A Christmas Anthology*. SPCK, London, 1994.

Wyndham-Lewis D. B. and Heseltine, G. C., *A Christmas Book: An Anthology for Moderns*. Dent, London, 1928.

Zualdi, Felix and Murphy, James H., *The Sacred Ceremonies of Low Mass*. Dublin, The Vincentian Fathers, 1961.